THE ITALIAN RENAISSANCE

harper ✟ torchbooks

*A reference-list of Harper Torchbooks, classified
by subjects, is printed at the end of this volume.*

J. H. Plumb

THE ITALIAN
RENAISSANCE

A Concise Survey of Its History and Culture

HARPER TORCHBOOKS ❧ *The Academy Library*
HARPER & ROW, PUBLISHERS
NEW YORK AND EVANSTON

THE ITALIAN RENAISSANCE

This book was first published in *The Horizon Book of the Renaissance* in 1961
by American Heritage Publishing Company, and is here reprinted by arrangement

First HARPER TORCHBOOK edition published 1965 by
Harper & Row Publishers, Incorporated
49 East 33rd Street
New York, N.Y., 10016

Library of Congress catalog card number: 61-11489

CONTENTS

I

THE DAWN OF THE

RENAISSANCE

The face of medieval Europe was scarred with the ruins of its past. In Rome itself, the Colosseum housed the barbarous Frangipani and their armed retainers, greedy, lawless, destructive; the Forum provided a quarry for churches and rough pasture for the cattle market, and beneath the broken columns of the temple of Castor and Pollux the bullocks awaited their slaughter. The Campagna was littered with the crumbling ruins of its aqueducts; the pavements of those splendid Roman roads were narrowed by the returning wilderness. Elsewhere scraps of walls, the ruins of arena, temple, and triumphal arch, sometimes embedded in the hovels and houses of a town struggling to regain its life or lost forever in the countryside, constantly reminded the man of the Middle Ages of the fleeting life of man, of the unknowable nature of Providence. For him the past was dead, and its relics but morals in stone, a terrible warning of the wickedness which God had punished.

The wealth that was wrung from the soil and the tenuous trade of those dark centuries was poured into the splendid barbaric churches, noble if grotesque, that soared to heaven in violation of all the harmonies of ancient art. Or it served a grimmer purpose, and from it grew the towering fortresses, the embattled towers, the walled cities that were a necessity in a society in which the clang of armor was as common as the church bell.

Yet relics there were, and the miracle is that so much survived the ravages of violence. The barbarian hordes had swept away the thin veneer of Roman culture in Northwestern Europe and broken the powerful web of trade, law, and government that had bound the Mediterranean world in unity. This breach, on which time had worked, was widened by the surge of Islam which swept across and absorbed not only Northern Africa, the islands of Sicily and Sardinia, but also the huge peninsula of Spain, and poured over the Pyrenees only to be checked on the plains of France. Under the hammer blows of Vikings, warrior colonists and traders by the sword, Europe and its culture had nearly bled to death. Violence, insecurity, and poverty reduced trade and city life to pitiful dimensions. Yet even in the worst of times, groups of peasants spread like a virus through the wastes and forests, colonizing those vast tracts of Europe which the Romans had dominated but never peopled.

Their lives were controlled by a warrior caste which attempted to give them protection, but battened on their labor; or by priests and monks who controlled the ritual of their existence and taught them that life was as fleeting as the crops they harvested. Men of this Western world lived simple, isolated, primitive lives in which pestilence, famine, and war marked the passage of the years.

Yet the past was never quite destroyed, the structure of society never utterly broken. Trade with the great civilizations of Islam and Byzantium transfused a little wealth into the shattered society of the West. More than wealth—ideas, too, could leap across the frontiers of hate and heresy to stimulate the cunning of men. So Byzantium lured men, warriors as well as traders, and so did the challenge of the Moslem world, which called the knights to battle and sanctified the blood-crazed warriors of Europe, offering them riches in life or glory in death.

This curious society of peasant and priest and warrior, which drew its strength from individual men rather than from nations or countries, was held together by the Catholic Church and by feudal law. The secular ideal, often expressed but rarely achieved, was of an ordered, graded society, unchanging and unchangeable, compounded of obligations and rights fixed by law, both written and customary. At all times the majority of men, including the most bloodstained baron, accepted unquestioningly the superior merits of the religious life; the liturgical worship of God and the contemplation of the spirit, by which man subordinated his nature and exorcised his desires, became a social ideal. And like all ideals dreamed of by many, it was attained by few. The institutions for its fulfillment were everywhere created, but frequently they served mere mundane ends. For the sake of power and wealth, men forgot their obligations, and found it sufficient to expiate their sins in age or defeat. Even for those who genuinely sought the ideal in the most ascetic monastery, the instincts of men broke through and compelled them to draw, to paint, and to sing for the glory of God.

In the darkest decades, there was a force at work—trade—which was inimical to this world of warriors, priests, and peasants. Trade drew Moslem, Jew, and Christian together; trade fattened towns, sometimes bred them. In so primitive a world, the personalities of kings and popes could lead either to strong government or to social anarchy; peace and good harvests could lift prosperity with outstanding rapidity; war and disease and famine could hold in check all progress, all growth, for a generation. At times it seemed as if the forces of expansion would lift Europe to a higher level of civility than it had known since the decay of Rome; at others that it would vanish and leave nothing but barbarism. In the eleventh century, towns and trade and craftsmanship grew rapidly. An intense interest in ancient learning, particularly in Aristotle, followed; the surging success of the Crusades promised new power and new prosperity. But the prospect faded and disaster followed. The Western Christians savaged the Byzantine Empire; the Moslem world revived under the powerful leadership of the Ottoman Turks; the scourge of the bubonic plague emptied the towns and reduced Europe's population by at least a third. A new death rather than a rebirth seemed Europe's prospect. Indeed, the dance of death became a threnody of life, haunting the imagination of men. Yet in the middle of the fourteenth century there were forces working like yeast in the economy and in the spirit of Italy. During the Renaissance these were to ferment and turn life into a new form, not only in Italy itself but throughout the Western world.

Throughout the Middle Ages, Italy never belonged wholly to Europe. The Romans had thoroughly colonized the land, creating an urban life which neither Goth nor Lombard nor Saracen ever totally destroyed. Feudalism was planted in Italy but never rooted deeply there. Gothic art achieved one or two outstanding successes, but never dominated the Italian imagination. Italy remained a prey of, not a breeding ground for, warriors. During the waves of invasion there were times when it seemed that Italian society might be destroyed or transmogrified. The hemorrhage of war weakened Italy's strength, emptied her towns, diminished her trade, and enfeebled all institutions save the Church of Rome, whose universality endowed it with some of the authority, if little of the strength, of the Caesars. But always there was trade, there was an urban life. When Belisarius landed in the sixth century at Naples with his Byzantine troops, intent on recapturing Italy for the Eastern Empire, his leading ally was a Syrian businessman, Antiochus. Aistolf's laws for the Lombards, about 750, legislate for merchants. A pair of Venetian traders, in 828, stole the relics of Saint Mark from Alexandria. By 836 there was at least one merchant, Semplicianus, rich enough to endow a monastery at Milan. Indeed, during these barbarous centuries, Venice was laying the foundations of its future greatness by exploiting the natural advantages that Italy possessed as the link between the primitive world of the North and the sophisticated East. The most valuable traffic was probably in men, women, and children, who were shipped to Alexandria where there was a ready slave market. Paid in coin, the Venetians then bought luxuries—the silks which the concubines of Charlemagne's court found so ravishing, the great silver dishes which might find their way into the ship-graves of chieftains by the northern seas, the papyrus that the papal Curia needed for its administration. As well as slaves, the Venetians traded the salt from their lagoon for the products of the Lombard plain. Nor was Venice the only mercantile community among Italian cities. Ships from Pisa, Genoa, and Amalfi ventured to the eastern Mediterranean, carrying pilgrims to the Holy Land, trading with the Greeks or the Moslems or the Jews, creating a spider's web of commerce. Yet progress was neither steady nor constant. Pirates infested the inland seas, war was endemic, and risks, like profits, were huge. Nor must the amount of trade be exaggerated; often it consisted of nothing more than a pedlar plodding dusty roads by the side of the Rhone, carrying his pack laden with eastern marvels to the rural fairs of Champagne.

Trade, however, was not the only catalyst at work in Italy and medieval Europe. The world of armed knights was not cheap; the courts of kings have never tolerated poverty; and though princes of the Church might preach self-denial, they rarely practiced it. As war became more highly technical, it became more costly; as kingdoms grew in strength, their administration needed larger funds; as the network of churches and monasteries honeycombed Europe, so the wealth and expenses of the Church became more vast. The result was that the merchants quickly found themselves in fresh and lush pastures. They became financiers. As with trade, so with finance, the seeding ground for the rest of Europe was Italy. The great banking street of London was, and still is, called Lombard Street after the Italian moneylenders who settled there in the thirteenth century. Of course, this high finance of popes, emperors, and kings could be as dangerous as trade. The Venetians rarely made any loans to a prince: the risk was too great and default too common. Yet in the handling of taxes, in the loans for war, in the purchased rights of justice, there were men who amassed fortunes. And by the High Middle Ages the structure of international finance, based on Italy, was as advanced as that of the ancient world. This helped to make Italian life more complex and more secular.

The burgeoning both of trade and of finance rested primarily on the growth of Europe's population. The great empty lands of Gaul, Britain, and Germany absorbed generation upon generation of men; in the struggle to conquer the forests, the marshes, and the wastes, few could be spared from the toil of the land save for prayer or for war. Although Italy was ravaged often, its thickly spread peasant population possessed remarkable powers of recuperation from famine, pestilence, and war, and this numerous people nourished crafts and industries. Wealth and commerce aided their growth, and the old walled Roman cities gave them protection. Cities, not states or kings or princes, dominated the land. The sole exception was the Pope, whose superiority in the hierarchy of universal power even emperors had, after bitter conflicts, reluctantly admitted. The popes intended both to protect the Patrimony of St. Peter and to prevent any secular ruler from achieving the hegemony of Italy. To achieve this aim they were rarely reluctant to call for their aid the warriors of France—an ominous precedent for the future. To check the Pope's territorial ambitions, some cities were not averse to asking on occasion for military help from the Emperor, to whom they owed a certain allegiance. It is true that the powers and rights of the Holy Roman Empire were more often ignored. Theoretically, the emperors claimed universal secular authority as the popes claimed universal spiritual power, but in practice the emperors' strength was based on the lands that they possessed in Germany, their estates in Italy, and a vast, ill-defined collection of rents, dues, and legal powers over the cities and states of Italy, the Netherlands, and parts of Burgundy. And any threat to the riches of Italy brought the imperial armies across the Alps. Invasion and war, sometimes desperate and tragic and bloody, threaded the history of Italy for a millennium, making her poets and philosophers dream of freedom, of unity, of peace. No great power ever succeeded for long, and the absence of a powerful state-system, the lack of any corpus of national law or secular jurisdiction, bred an openness to political experiment that was in itself a powerful stimulus to the new age which dawned in Italy toward the end of the fourteenth century, an age which was dominated by the city-state that was born in the violence and anarchy of medieval Italy.

Trade, high finance, a large and partially urbanized population, quickening industry, the absence of a deeply rooted all-powerful political structure—all of these were seminal. There were, however, other forces—equally important, if less measurable—that were needed to change the whole life of Italy at the Renaissance as certainly and as dramatically as the Industrial Revolution changed the face of Britain in the late eighteenth century. Ideas, like heresy, traveled in the Middle Ages along the lines of trade. From Byzantium, from Islam, from the prosperous and flourishing lands of France, Burgundy, and the Flemish towns came ideas in art, in technology, in science, and in philosophy. And even in the most barbarous times, cultivated Italians never forgot the great traditions of their imperial past nor their splendid achievements in literature. Throughout the Middle Ages the classics had been copied, studied frequently for their moral virtues, occasionally enjoyed for themselves.

Monks appreciated Horace as well as Seneca, and even Ovid was not unknown to the cloister. There were high points of excitement and discovery. The recovery of many of Aristotle's works in the twelfth and early thirteenth centuries, from Arabic sources, created an intellectual ferment in scholastic circles. As secular life grew in complexity and stability and urbanity, the laws of Justinian became the object of devoted research, and long before the Renaissance, Roman ideas of law, of order, and of government had permeated Italian city life. This complex society, never far from barbarism yet close to civility, threw up men of great intellectual stature and brilliant literary gifts. Long before the Renaissance dawned, Saint Thomas Aquinas had provided a philosophic argument for dogma that was to serve men for century after century. Dante, the Florentine, produced the first great poem in Italian—a poem that is medieval in spirit but modern in technique—and Petrarch, who followed, showed that Dante's achievement was not likely to remain unique. These were but the brightest stars in a luminous firmament.

Europe of the Middle Ages was not a closed world. The Crusades had ripped open the Near East and given the hordes of warriors a taste of sophisticated, cultured society which previously had only been the experience of merchants and pilgrims. And Italy was the door through which the Crusaders passed. There had been more distant seekings, too. Marco Polo had reached Peking; links, unfortunately to prove as fragile as gossamer, had been made with the long-lost Nestorian Christians of India and China. At one time it seemed as if the Great Khan himself might turn Christian and link Europe with the eastern seas. The glimpse of the wider world proved brief—the Khan remained a Buddhist, the Chinese threw off Mongol control, and Ottomans swept the Christian powers out of Asia Minor, seized the Balkans, and threatened Italy itself. Yet this ebb and flow of European power interlocked the Christian and

Moslem worlds. Methods and materials passed from one to the other. At the splendid court in Sicily of Frederick II, it was an Arab who taught geography and presented the Emperor with a silver sphere on which the map of the world was drawn. Indeed, at that court the Renaissance itself seemed at hand. Frederick, ruthless, amoral, violent, a realist in politics as in philosophy, might have been an uncle of Cesare Borgia. Although he was the Holy Roman Emperor, possessing vast lands and vaster rights beyond the Alps, the core of Frederick's strength and power lay in his kingdom of Sicily, which contained most of southern Italy as well as the island itself. Here he introduced laws based on Justinian's code, fostered city life, and favored the bourgeoisie. He patronized the arts; encouraged literature, poetry, science; kept an astrologer; dabbled in alchemy; brought together a menagerie of rare animals and an exotic collection of mistresses. He lived flamboyantly and realistically and delighted in the creative activities of man. But he was a portent, not a man of his time. Legends festooned his name, and they called him *stupor mundi* as much from awe as from flattery. The delight of his court in literature and in philosophic inquiry, the efficiency of his administration, the energy of his diplomacy, and above all the openness of his mind to all ideas, whether Moslem or Christian or pagan, struck a rare chord in thirteenth-century Europe. Yet about him and his courtiers there is still an air of barbarism, a lack of sophistication, even of experience, that makes his world, in truth if not in appearance, closer to that of Charlemagne or Otto I than that of Lorenzo de' Medici or Lodovico Sforza.

By the time of Lorenzo and Lodovico, Italy had changed fundamentally and dramatically, and this change is rightly called the Renaissance. In Rome broad streets had been driven through the chaotic slums that crouched amid the rubbish of antiquity. A new city had arisen about the Vatican, and the plans for the huge Basilica of St. Peter were slowly taking shape. The palaces of the cardinals proclaimed the tastes, the interests, the sophistications of this new age. As in Rome, so in Florence. The great towers in which families had sought refuge during the furious vendettas of the Middle Ages had been razed. In their place stood the opulent homes of patrician families—Strozzi, Medici, Rucellai, and the rest. These great houses were designed according to the austere classical harmonies that the great architect of the Renaissance—Brunelleschi—had made fashionable. Out in the Tuscan countryside the first villas of modern times rivaled those of Augustan Rome. The style as well as the decoration of these buildings was in sharp and vivid contrast to the Gothic which so many men and women of the Renaissance thoughtlessly despised, not realizing the extent of their debt to their recent past. But such unawareness was scarcely surprising, for their age was astonishingly fresh, and the achievements of the fifteenth century as remarkable as they were original. Historians, concerned with origins and remote influences, stress how deeply interlocked this age of the Renaissance was with the medieval world: how much it owed to Flanders, to Paris, to Byzantium. True as this may be, it also distorts reality by the nature of its emphasis. It would be folly to underestimate the creative strength and originality of fifteenth-century Italy. This stretched far beyond architecture, dramatic though the structural changes of the Italian cities were. In sculpture and in painting the change was, perhaps, more profound. In both these arts there had been precursors—Giotto, the great Florentine painter, Duccio, the Sienese, and Andrea Pisano, the sculptor—and the break with the past was neither so sharp nor so vivid as in building. The achievement, however, was far greater. For the next four centuries the themes, the traditions, the techniques, and the preoccupations of the artists of fifteenth-century Italy were to dominate Western Europe. The roll call of their names—Fra Angelico, Bellini, Botticelli, Donatello, Ghiberti, Leonardo,

Lippi, Mantegna, Michelangelo, Pollaiuolo, Signorelli, and Verrocchio, a list that could be doubled with scarcely any loss of
quality—speaks for itself: such a constellation of artistic genius,
spread over a mere century and a half, would alone make this
age of the Renaissance one of the great epochs of human
achievement.

Yet art was only one aspect of the brilliance of Renaissance
Italy, which created an image of man, a vision of human excellence, that *still* lies at the heart of the Western tradition.
Rarely achieved, it has nevertheless haunted men like a mirage.
The Italians, particularly the Florentines, revered antiquity—its
wisdom, its grace, its philosophy, and its literature. Sensitive
and deep-thinking men had done so, of course, ever since the
Roman world had crumbled into decay; in monastic schools
and universities Plato, as well as Aristotle, had been studied
intensively. Yet such knowledge had been largely part of the
private world of scholars. At the time of the Renaissance these
humanistic studies spread through the upper and middle ranks
of society and became a formidable part of the education of
those who were to wield power and authority. The timely invention of the printing press not only multiplied the works of
antiquity so that they were readily available to hundreds of
thousands of men and women, but also helped to create a public
for their study. What had been private became public, and a
study of the classical heritage became a necessity for a gentleman; indeed, his familiarity with the classics was the hallmark
of civility. A man might still be a warrior, a priest, a merchant,
with a professional outlook and professional mores, yet if he
wished to be regarded as the complete man, *l'uomo universale,*
more was expected of him. He needed to be well-bred, and the
breeding of a gentleman was defined by Italians of the Renaissance. They insisted on a refinement of taste, an ease of manner,
combined with a capacity for manly pursuits, a knowledge of
the classics, an acquaintance with history and philosophy, an

appreciation of music, painting, architecture, and sculpture, a connoisseurship of the rare and the beautiful whether they might be books, jewels, coins, or scraps of antiquity. All of these interests were to be lightly borne, without pedantry or excessive professionalism. This was the image that Castiglione created in his famous book, *The Courtier*—an image which was drawn from the knowledge he acquired of men such as Lorenzo de' Medici and Federigo da Montefeltro.

To acquire, let alone indulge, such sophisticated tastes required money, for education in so many disciplines and interests, even if superficial, took time, and no one could patronize the arts without wealth. As patronage grew competitive, the arts themselves became more costly. Renaissance society was designed for rich men, rich cities, rich popes. To maintain so vast an expenditure required an active and most profitable commerce; to indulge it a prodigious concentration of costly talent was necessary. And the Italian cities possessed both. Venice, Florence, Milan, and Rome were full of exceedingly rich men, and money, which was the base of all Renaissance achievement, nurtured genius. The transmutation of gold into works of art was the result of a complex social process, the marriage between aristocratic extravagance and bourgeois ambition. The aristocrats of medieval Europe did not vanish overnight; they still lived on, maintaining their sense of caste, providing a snobbish goal toward which the rich merchant could direct his social ambition. The patricians of Florence, Milan, or Venice might be merchants, but they wished to live like nobles. In Italy of the Renaissance, therefore, aristocratic and bourgeois attitudes fused to create a pattern of life, a tradition of social expression that was to be adopted by societies of the West as the wealth of the New World and of the Indies poured into their cities. Commercial capitalism, struggling in the framework of feudalism, learned, through Italy, not only how to express itself in art and learning, but also how to make an art of life itself.

It is a sobering thought that the great Italian achievements in almost every sphere of intellectual and artistic activity took place in a world of violence and war. Cities were torn by feud and vendetta: Milan warred against Venice, Florence against Pisa, Rome against Florence, Naples against Milan. Alliances were forged only to be broken, the countryside was constantly scarred by pillage, rapine, and battle, and in this maelstrom the old bonds of society were broken and new ones forged. After a brief period of peace, in the second half of the fifteenth century, the confusion and carnage grew worse through the great French invasions of Charles VIII, Louis XII, and Francis I, a time of agony that did not end till the dreadful sack of Rome in 1527 by the Holy Roman Emperor, Charles V. Yet this violence worked like yeast in the thought of men, and profoundly influenced the way they were to regard problems of power and government for hundreds of years. They ceased to look for answers to the fate of man in the dogmas of the Church. They searched the histories of antiquity for precedents that might guide them to the truth, but they also sought to explain, as Machiavelli did, the world in which they lived by what they knew to be the nature of man. Indeed, it was during the Renaissance in Italy that many men came to feel that truth was elusive, a mood afterward strengthened by the discovery of the world beyond Europe. The old dogmatic certainties did not vanish at once, and the habit of trying to nail truth down by argument from fundamental principles was not lightly cast aside. Some of the most original minds, however, particularly Machiavelli and Leonardo da Vinci, sought truth not in argument but in observation. Machiavelli brooded on men and events, on the effects of political action and on the consequence of chance; Leonardo grew preoccupied with the flow of water, the flight of birds, the formation of rocks. The growth of ideas and the development of mental attitudes are difficult to pinpoint in the course of history, but this, at least, can be said: the men of the Renaissance, by the range of their inquiries, by the freshness of their skepticism, and by the sharpness of their observation, gave impetus to, and helped to acquire intellectual acceptance for, the search for truth on earth instead of in heaven.

Artistic expression, intellectual inquiry, social attainments—the Renaissance enriched all these things in an original and creative way. Its influence spread throughout Europe and continued for centuries. It was the work of hundreds of gifted men and a score of remarkable cities—Vicenza, Rimini, Ferrara, Urbino, Mantua, Parma, and the rest all made their contributions. They had their artists, philosophers, poets, and craftsmen of genius and distinction, yet the full force of the Renaissance flowed most strongly in four cities—Florence, Milan, Rome, and Venice. Florence, a very small city by modern standards, cradled the Renaissance and produced an astonishing array of genius which Rome and Milan, both far richer than Florence, patronized. The full tide of the Renaissance reached Venice late, but it lingered there longer, creating an island of delight in a world made brutal by the new clash of religious ideologies as the Reformation broke Europe asunder. Neither Reformation nor Counter Reformation, nor the economic decline of Italy, brought on by the discovery of the New World, could check the spread of the Renaissance. Its ideas and its achievements ran like an ineradicable dye through the fabric of Europe, and its monuments have become a part of the world's heritage.

II

THE PRINCE

AND THE STATE

"Horror waits on princes," wrote Webster, the Elizabethan dramatist for whom the bloodstained annals of Italy had a compulsive fascination. Certainly, the way to power was strewn with corpses; men murdered their wives, wives poisoned their husbands, brother slaughtered brother, family raged against family, city sacked city. In 1402 the chief members of the ruling house of Lodi were burned alive on the public square; at Bologna in 1445 the people, enraged by the slaughter of their favorite family, the Bentivoglio, hunted down their enemies and nailed their steaming hearts to the doors of the Bentivoglio's palace, as a token of their love.

Yet Bologna was a tranquil city compared to many, and even bloodless when matched with Foligno; there a noble—Pietro Rasiglia—cuckolded by his prince, took his vengeance. He flung his faithless wife from the turrets of his castle and killed two brothers of the prince. Retribution rapidly followed. The whole Rasiglia clan, men, women, and children, were butchered and chopped up; their joints, hung like meat, were paraded through the streets. Of course, the ghoulish chroniclers liked to heighten the horror, and their macabre imaginations rioted in sadistic fantasy. Yet all allowances made, politics became a murderous game in which death in bed came only to the skillful or the lucky. The savagery used by men in pursuit of power was due to the nature of society and the prizes which it offered.

The city-states of Italy had won their independence by play-ing off the two greatest powers of medieval Europe—the Papacy and the Empire. In theory, the Pope ruled men's souls, the Emperor their bodies; the facts accorded ill with theory. The Church had acquired property which no emperor or king could match; its real estate, its pecuniary rights—first fruits, Peter's pence, and the like—made it formidably rich, rich enough to challenge the Empire and to claim the supremacy of the spiritual over the temporal power. Yet bishops were princes as well as bishops; abbots and their monasteries owed feudal obligations on their lands. The great baronage of the Empire bred too many sons to view the Church's dependence on Rome with equanimity. Who should or should not select or confirm the bishops in their rights became a vital matter for emperors. And although the great struggle between the Empire and the Papacy expressed itself in the language of theology, its roots were mundane enough—land, money, power. Behind the Papacy stood the great estate of the clergy, formidable in numbers, in learning, and in authority; the Emperor had his own resources. His major strength was drawn from his lands and rights in Germany, Austria, and the Netherlands, but he was also King of Lombardy and, as such, possessed important and valuable lands in Northern Italy; yet his presence was rare in these ter-ritories, and his enemies flourished at his expense. The chief of these was the Papacy, rendered strong and inflexible by the great reforming popes of the twelfth and thirteenth centuries.

The Papacy, conscious of its God-given role in the *respublica Christiana,* had not been reluctant to encourage the revolt of the Italian communes, any more than it had hesitated to call to its aid the ferocious Norman barons, to help it in its conflict with the emperors. This great struggle unleashed on town and village and countryside the fratricidal war between the Pope's party, the *parte Guelfa,* and the Emperor's, the *parte Ghibel-*

lina, which continued long after the defeat of the Hohenstaufen emperors had destroyed the hopes of the Ghibellines. It left behind two poles of feeling about which passion and anger and rivalry could crystallize—often to the point of absurdity, as when the Ghibellines of Milan tore down the Christ from the high altar in the Cathedral of Cremona because His face was turned to His shoulder in the manner of a Guelph. Yet the great conflict between Pope and Emperor left behind more than a tradition of internecine war. It unleashed chaos; an anarchy of power in which the strong devoured the weak, in which trivial wars, scarcely more significant than riots, alternated with struggles that involved the lives of thousands. From 1350 to 1450 Italy scarcely knew a month, let alone a year, of peace. Yet during this time the great states—Florence, Milan, Naples, Venice—emerged as the arbiters of Italy's destiny. None powerful enough to overthrow the others, they lived in an uneasy equilibrium of power that lasted for nearly fifty years until, in 1494, welcomed by Milan, the French king invaded Italy to assert his dynastic claims. Wars more terrible and more violent than Italy had ever known ravaged the land and turned Lombardy into a cockpit in the struggle between the Hapsburg emperors and the French kings, a struggle that lasted until the sack of Rome in 1527, when Charles V brutally reasserted the Imperial power and tied the destiny of Italy to the house of Hapsburg.

In war or in peace, in freedom or in subjection, the towns grew, and in growing changed the nature of their government, sliding from hopeful democracy into greedy oligarchy. They varied greatly in size and power—a few like Florence, nearly a hundred thousand strong, a hive of trade and manufacture, and many like Orvieto of about twenty thousand, busy market towns of farmers, shopkeepers, and artisans. Yet, great or small, they had each undergone a novel political experience—the flowering of a qualified democracy in the midst of feudalism. Within these cities the *popolo*—not the people but the members of craft guilds—had acquired power and taken over or devised their own institutions of government. Usually they possessed no written authority or fundamental constitution; they exercised power, solved their problems, *ad hoc*. They represented not only the wealth and the enterprise of the city, but also that oligarchy of families which could hold and maintain authority. Force, and the consent of their immediate supporters, was the basis of their government. There was rarely unity in any commune—the nobility both of the surrounding countryside, known as the *contado*, which acknowledged the authority of the city, or of the city itself, had long been divided by feuds and rivalries before the division between Guelph and Ghibelline gave their hatreds a sharper edge. And athough the artisans and merchants dominated the life of the city they frequently needed the skill and the training of the nobility both in diplomacy and in war. Furthermore, the unformalized nature of these city constitutions enabled men seeking power to manipulate the quasi-democratic methods of government, as the Medici were to do with supreme skill in Florence. And the relics of the nobility, or in the large towns the great merchant oligarchs, had little difficulty in acquiring the leadership and the control of seemingly "popular" movements. Hence there was a pronounced tendency for all communes to drift, either secretly or openly, to the despotism of a family or a clique. This was the ground swell that was to lift the Renaissance prince to power.

Chance, however, in the shape of the great bubonic plague that ravished Italy in the middle of the fourteenth century, also took a hand. Men and women died like flies, and death ate up the cities more rapidly than the countryside. Chronicler after chronicler tells of the empty streets, the pillaged houses, the yawning pits in the graveyards, and the resulting poverty from the decay of trade. In this blighted world it was naturally easier for tyranny to flourish.

Yet plague or no plague, tyranny probably would have thrived. From the earliest days of these communes, force and expediency had governed all. Their urbanism had been as militant and as aggressive as any nationalism. They had seized villages and lesser towns by force; and war had been the life-blood of their growth. A small town such as Orvieto, perched on its impregnable fortress of rock, quickly absorbed great tracts of countryside, stretching south to the Lake of Bolsena, westward to the coast, eastward to the Tiber, and north almost to Lake Trasimeno—almost, because greater cities than Orvieto were expanding too. Siena and Perugia wanted the territory that Orvieto coveted. Neither was without enemies on its own northern borders. Florence hated Siena and attacked or courted Perugia according to her need. So war was endemic, and the citizens were constantly marching out to do battle with their neighbors.

The further dimension of diplomacy, with the vast para-phernalia of chicanery and pressure and secrecy, found its breeding ground in the rivalries and conflicts of these city-states, for what was true of Orvieto, Siena, Perugia, and Florence was equally true of the cities of the Lombard plan or the Patrimony of St. Peter. Only in the south, in the kingdoms of Naples and of Sicily, was the conflict of cities held in check by the rule of hereditary monarchy. The Papacy, which might have given coherence to the Patrimony of St. Peter, had been transferred to Avignon in 1309, where it remained until 1378. From then until 1417 the Great Schism provided yet additional causes for division and strife not only in the Papal States, but also throughout Italy. And it was not until 1421 that Martin V re-established the Papacy firmly and securely at Rome. The Emperor, after the defeat of the last of the Hohenstaufen, lacked the power to influence, let alone control, Lombardy's political development. Hence the appetites of the city-states for their neighbors' lands went unchecked, and war was constant. And not only war—so was treason, murder, and plot, for this reason. Some states lacked constitutions, they were without the constitutional formalization of social, economic, and political power that was sanctioned by tradition or by law. Power was captured by groups, by interrelated families, sometimes depending on oligarchic, sometimes on popular, support, and occasionally on the help of other city-states and, in time, on foreign invasion. Exiles from all states abounded, to become the instruments of aggression: murder, trickery, and civil war were accepted elements of political activity. Gradually, as war diminished the localization of power, the great city-states emerged. Florence battered down Pisa and Pistoia; Venice absorbed Padua and Verona; Milan ate up Pavia and Lodi; by skillful alliances a few smaller states—Ferrara, Mantua, and others—survived to act as pawns in the checkerboard of power. Such states were too large and too rich to rely on the citizen army, which had been sufficient in the earlier days when the enemy was but a day's march away. Also, war was becoming too technical for simple peasants and workers. The cities had the need for, and the money to hire, the professional soldiers —the condottieri—who roamed Italy in order to ravage a living from its people. As the wily Venetians realized, the condottieri prevented armed power from being placed in the hands of a citizen or his faction; and so it became a fixed principle of Venetian administration that no Venetian born could command its army. At first the condottieri were foreign—Sir John Hawkwood, an Englishman, had a famous band of ravishers, the White Company. Soon the tyrants of petty states put themselves and their citizens out for hire. Some, like the Montefeltro of Urbino, kept their states, their heads, and their reputations; others, like Francesco Sforza, won a duchy; most died violently, executed, murdered, killed in battle. They lived for hire, but they could not be trusted, since bought troops meant treacherous troops. Always the danger loomed of a condottiere turning against the state that employed him. This the Venetians and the Florentines realized clearly enough, and they saw to it that the camps of their condottieri were riddled with spies. The use of hired professional armies reduced violence even though it increased treachery, for no captain wished to waste his greatest asset—his fighting men. As a result, battles were rare, sieges infinitely prolonged. And increasingly, to the alarms and rumors of war and conspiracy were added the deliberate exaggeration and the hidden subterfuges of diplomacy.

Diplomacy as we know it arose in Italy of the Renaissance. It grew strong in the fifteenth century through the equilibrium of power created by the three great northern states of Italy— Milan, Venice, and Florence. It appealed to the leaders of these mercantile societies. They enjoyed and believed in the efficacy of hard bargaining, nor were they unaware of the merits of partnership for the destruction of rivals (and partners need supervision as well as persuasion). The collection of intelligence, the assessment of personalities and contingencies, was early the stock in trade of bankers. The application of these commercial techniques to the service of the state was effortlessly made. Every Venetian abroad was expected to spy for his country. Nor was intelligence required solely for the purpose of foreign affairs; internally it was of equal if not greater importance. The fear of tyrants intensified their suspicion as well as their cruelty; thus their citizens and followers were encouraged to spy and to betray. Such behavior was not peculiar to despotisms: in Venice men were encouraged to report anonymously their suspicions of their neighbors. These calumnies were meticulously sifted, at times with the help of the rack and the boot, by the republic's inquisitors. Elsewhere fear took on more fantastic shapes, and friends, relations, and children of tyrants lived on a volcano of violence that could erupt on the slightest suspicion. Naturally, such insecurity bred a desire to survive that overrode all claims to loyalty or affection, and frequently poison or the dagger momentarily cleared a state of its bloodstained ruler. Yet such actions and attitudes were an accepted part of the political and military life.

The frequency of assassination, the perennial plots, the constant vicissitudes, encouraged superstition and a romantic view of Fate. Men felt themselves to be the prey of strange destinies and turned to astrologers and magicians to strengthen their hope, to check despair, and to help them meet the uncertain future with confidence. The stars were studied as intensely as diplomatic dispatches, as a guide to action; and superstitious dread threaded the daily course of men's lives. Even the popes felt more secure in their faith when the heavens were propitious. Julius II fixed the date of his coronation on the advice of his astrologers, and Paul III arranged his consistories at the dictates of the stars.

The ever-present sense of death and danger heightened instinct as well as superstition. The possession of power, naked and absolute, removed the barriers for its gratification, no matter how quaint the desire might be. At the courts of the despots sexual license was as common as treachery. And in the rampages of the flesh, as in the pursuit of power, the popes were second to none. The princes and the republics of the Renaissance lived in a dangerous, excitable, and exciting world of power. Morality was not involved, only success. But, of course, only a few princes, nobles, and merchants were concerned in any state. The mass of the people eschewed office, and the disasters of government troubled them only in military defeat.

Yet it would be wrong to consider the tyrants of Italy as concerned only with the pursuit of power by the most cruel methods. Many were intelligent, some sensitive; all desired fame. Since fame involved outward expression—buildings, statuary, art, pag-

eants, tourneys, and even public benefactions—patronage, in its
widest aspects, was an illustration of power, or rather of social
and political grandeur. Splendor added stature to the Doge as
well as the Pope, and the Visconti with their Cathedral of Milan
and their Certosa at Pavia glorified their state as well as their
dynasty. Display became a part of the art of government, and
the wealth of Italy permitted an extravagance that would not
have been unbecoming to an ancient Roman emperor. Pageantry
was also a part of the aristocratic tradition, but the riches of the
Medici, the Sforza, the Gonzaga, or the Este, and the skill of
their painters and sculptors, raised this art to an intenser level.
The tourneys which celebrated the wedding of Beatrice d'Este
and Lodovico Sforza were prolonged, extravagant, drenched in
mythology, a vast spectacle that took months to prepare and days
to enact. And for this Leonardo da Vinci directed his genius to
the design of the costumes. The power of princes and the glory
of cities could be expressed less ephemerally. All raised monuments to their greatness in buildings, in painting, and in sculpture. Leonardo da Vinci sought the patronage of Cesare Borgia
as well as Lodovico Sforza; Raphael began his career in the
most bloodstained and power-ravaged city of Italy—Perugia. The
patronage of tyrants took delight in all that gratified the mind
as well as the senses of men. Exquisite and extravagant food,
fabulous and sumptuous clothing, delicate and intricate jewelry,
masterpieces of craftsmanship in silver and gold, lightened the
strain and soothed the anxieties of princes. So did the memorials
of antiquity, the broken torsos, the green, encrusted bronzes, the
coins and medallions, which the earth yielded. Books were novel
not only in their contents but also in their new printed form,
and it was not long before they became as worthy of collection
as the illustrated manuscripts of the recent past. The animate
world also distracted the mind and ennobled the possessor.
Strange animals or misshapen men were collected like curios.
Popes and kings, cardinals and princes, outbid each other to per-

suade the great in art, letters, and science to join their entourage; rarely has so great a premium been placed on men of creative ability. These strange courts of princes—so close to violence, yet so alive to beauty, so transient in power, yet so permanent in expression—need a closer focus, both the best and the worst.

At Mantua, high above the Piazza Sordello, swings an iron cage; throughout the fourteenth and fifteenth century it was usually occupied by a dead or dying man. The grim, embattled palaces of the Bonacolsi and the Gonzaga provided a fitting background to the sagas of their princes. The lords of Mantua had their quota of fratricide, of treasonable sons and murderous uncles, of wives caught in adultery and killed for their crime. Its citizens, as well as its princes, had their times of horror, their years of tribulation. Like all city-states it was born in feudal anarchy and nurtured by inter-urban strife. Gifted with a superb natural strength (on three sides the Mincio swells out into large, wide lakes that proved difficult to probe), Mantua quickly dominated the surrounding countryside and held it against the most formidable assaults of its combined enemies. Still, it is doubtful whether it could have survived but for the aid of Venice. It was too strong and too remote for Venice to absorb, yet its powerful princes were an excellent buffer against their common enemy, Milan. So the Venetians hired the Gonzaga as condottieri and, to pay them, ceded Lombard towns that were too weak to maintain their independence and too poor for Venice to covet. The Gonzaga were too clever to allow a tradition of dependence on Venice to develop, and from time to time they sold their skill to the rulers of Milan. The balance of power kept Mantua independent, and the needs of Venice or Milan made it rich. Violent though its history was, it enjoyed more peace and greater security than was the common lot of Italian cities. The unruly, battle-scarred Gonzaga were never mere condottieri; they governed as strongly as they fought. Under Lodovico Gonzaga, in spite of plague and pestilence and flood, trade in wool and silks flourished, and the population grew to forty thousand or more. Money from war and trade was spent not only to delight the eye, but also to train the mind. Opportunities for pageantry proved frequent enough. Pius II called a council there in 1459 to declare a Crusade against the Turks. In 1474 the King of Denmark paid a state visit and found a royal welcome. Powerful neighbors—the Sforza from Milan, the Este from Ferrara—expected and received extravagant hospitality. The births and marriages and deaths of Gonzaga princes were celebrated with appropriate solemnity and expense. So were their triumphs: few public occasions matched the reception of Francesco Gonzaga, the first cardinal of his house, a prince of the Church at seventeen and a symbol of his family's greatness.

As became Renaissance princes, the Gonzaga sought a permanent expression for their wealth and power and destiny. Lodovico (1414–1478) was, perhaps, the most gifted of his family and possessed abundantly those wide-ranging tastes and abilities that were so much admired in his day. He embodied the skill and decision of a man of action with the sensitivity of a scholar. He proved himself ruthless in war, adept in diplomacy, yet more generous toward his treacherous brother Carlo than was usual in a despot, a sign of that human warmth which infused his private life and his artistic sensibilities. By 1460 he had persuaded Andrea Mantegna to make Mantua his permanent home and to become his court painter. The result was a splendid series of frescoes that still adorn the Camera degli Sposi in the Castello of Mantua; other frescoes have been destroyed, and pictures that were painted for Lodovico dispersed, but what remains is one of the great achievements of the Renaissance. As with painting, so with architecture: for Lodovico's taste was sure. He employed Alberti—a man of universal genius and a leading Florentine figure in the Classical revival—to design his churches, and urged Mantuans to give generously so that plans for Sant' Andrea could become a reality, which, as Lodovico said, "from its vast size and noble simplicity should be superior to any building of the kind in the leading cities of Italy, and worthy to stand beside the magnificence of Rome herself." Huge buildings, sumptuous palaces, brilliant paintings—these were the common extension of a prince's greatness. Lodovico, however, was a man of wider and deeper sympathies. He encouraged philosophers and poets to stay at his court. Pico della Mirandola, Platina, Poliziano, Ognibene, Guarino da Verona, and Filelfo all, at one time or another, brought distinction to the Mantuan court. Lodovico himself took a delight in books; he collected not only manuscripts of the classics, but also of Dante, Petrarch, and Boccaccio, and employed the most gifted craftsmen to illustrate their books.

The width of Lodovico's interests was due partly to his native genius and partly also to his education, for it was in the education of princes that Mantua made one of its most remarkable contributions to the Renaissance. Lodovico's father had established the great humanist Vittorino da Feltre at Mantua. Vittorino's ideas were to influence European education profoundly for centuries. He believed that education should concern itself with the body as well as the mind, with the senses as well as the spirit. Wrestling, fencing, swimming, and riding alternated with hours devoted to Virgil, Homer, Cicero, and Demosthenes. Luxury was eschewed, and Vittorino educated the poor with the rich. Nor was he prejudiced about the sexes; the Gonzaga princesses enjoyed the same extensive education as the princes. Above all, he encouraged the belief that individual greatness was part of the nature of man, and a desirable part, one that was in no way in opposition to the obligations which men had to their fellow men. To Vittorino the virtues were innate; they were human. Although a devout Christian and insistent on regular religious practices, he nevertheless cherished an optimistic view of man's capacities. Certainly in Lodovico, as in the great Federigo da Montefeltro, Vittorino found an apt pupil, and the traditions which he helped to create kept the Gonzaga from gross money for their campaigns of revenge. And the oppression which Perugians suffered too often lured them into thinking that any change of master might be for the better.

Here are but a few examples of Perugia's tribulations, of the curse of blood that seemed to its great chronicler Matarazzo to be the city's fate.

In 1488 the Baglioni and their enemies the Oddi fought a pitched battle in the Piazza, and the governors of the city were helpless to stop it. In 1491 the Baglioni strung up before the Palazzo dei Priori 130 men, supporters of the Oddi, who had found their way into the city. Shortly after this the Baglioni were only saved by the bravery and skill of Simonetto, a boy of eighteen, who held a narrow street with a few followers until they were nearly hacked to pieces. Then came the great betrayal in which four of the leading Baglioni were slaughtered in the beds—including Simonetto. Between 1520 and 1535 practic all who were left of the Baglioni were either publicly execu or murdered by each other. Nor were these fratricidal vendettas the only horror that the Perugians had to suffer. War was waged in their *contado* with a ferocity unusual for the fifteenth century, for the Baglioni, as condottieri, did not believe in half measures. And to give an additional taste of horror, the plague found in Perugia a happy playground—between 1424 and 1486 there were eight severe epidemics.

Violence and sickness, suffering and death, made the Perugians susceptible to the more evangelistic expressions of religious fervor. The slaughters by, or of, the Baglioni were usually followed by days of solemn ritual and purification. On one occasion the cathedral was washed with wine and reconsecrated; on another over thirty altars were erected in the Piazza, and Mass was continuously solemnized. It is not, therefore surprising that the vivid preaching of Fra Bernardino of Siena found a fruitful soil in Perugia. The people of the city responded eagerly to his denunciations of the vanity of all earthly life. He condemned the crimes

excesses and saved Mantua from the terrible sufferings w
were so frequently the lot of other Italian cities. And Lod
was as lucky in his children and his grandchildren as Ma
was in its dynasty. His son Federigo proved himself as ski
a condottiere, as wily a diplomat, and as sensitive a patro
his father, but it was his grandson Francesco and his wife,
bella d'Este, who lifted the court of Mantua to its highest fa

There were few among the lesser cities which enjoyed s
serenity as Mantua or were led by so able a man. Ferrara un
the Este, Bologna under the Bentivoglio, and Urbino under
Montefeltro were perhaps its nearest rivals, but the common
of cities was more grievous, their tyrants more terrible. Orvie
in little more than fifty years, was sacked and ravaged eig
times, and sacked and ravaged with a brutality that was exce
tional even for those murderous times. Yet even in an age whi
had grown immune to violence, the thought of Perugia and
tyrants made men quail.

The cities of the papal states experienced the most unfortuna
fate of all the Italian communes. The absence of the popes
Avignon had given an opportunity for princely anarchy to flou
ish; the Great Schism had encouraged lawlessness and rapin
and the return of the popes to Rome merely led to punitive wa
Both by geographical position and by reason of its size, Perug
was regarded as one of the most important cities of the Patrimon
By the middle of the fifteenth century its history was steeped i
bloodshed that none other could equal. Chroniclers delighted i
exaggeration and enjoyed recounting bloodcurdling deeds, y
after making every allowance, the Perugian story is horrifyin
in its utter cruelty and in its wanton disregard of human suffe
ing. The great families, who with their armed ruffians rage
and stormed and slaughtered in its streets and churches, faile
to exterminate each other; some always seemed to escape, t
live to plot revenge. Naturally, the cities that feared Perugi
were ready to succor them and to provide them with arms an

of its citizens, called them to repentance, reconciled enemies, and made a large bonfire of worldly delights in a great act of public repentance. The results of Bernardino proved as fleeting as were the reconciliations of the Baglioni and the Oddi later in the century, yet this thread of religious revivalism, of sensational open-air preaching, of the sudden need for public repentance, was not an unusual theme in city life of fifteenth-century Italy— it was a common response to the insecurities created by war and pestilence and crime.

Although the constant strife proved inimical to trade, although the population declined, these things failed to kill the vigorous artistic life of Perugia. In the midst of the turmoils, paintings of exceptional beauty were produced: Perugino and Raphael shared the city with the Baglioni and the Oddi. Perugino's frescoes of quiet, ecstatic saints, and Bonfiglio's charming, tender, personal vision of the merciful Madonna, provided the background for fratricidal slaughter in a piazza reeking with blood and festooned with the grotesque shapes of slaughtered youths and men. At no other place were the dark and the light of Renaissance life brought to a stranger contrast.

Sensitive, thoughtful men realized that this was a world like none other. They searched the histories of antiquity—Livy, Suetonius, Plutarch—looking for the keys that would unlock for them the problems of princes and of cities. What made men succeed? Or fail? Why did some cities grow great and rich only to dissipate it all in war and rebellion? Why did free citizens become the prey of professional thugs? What were the causes of tyranny? Was tyranny bad? Did cities have a natural life like men—youth, maturity, age? And were learning, art, and the practice of humanism bound up with the nature of institutions? Did philosophers make the best citizens? They ransacked antiquity, read again and again Plato and Aristotle and, above all, Cicero, who seemed to demonstrate more clearly than any other the virtues of a philosopher at large in civic life. What they did

not turn to was theology, to Saint Thomas Aquinas, to Saint
Ambrose, or to Saint Jerome. The theological way of thinking
about men and events was as alien to them as a salon painting
to Picasso. The key to their problems they knew to be rooted
in the lives and actions of men, not in universal mysteries or the
attributes of God. Consequently, there is an astonishing freshness
about the historians and the political philosophers of the Renaissance, and, as with the painters and sculptors, the greatest by
far were the Florentines, and the greatest of the Florentines was
Niccolò Machiavelli, whose speculations about the nature of
men's political actions are as remote from the thinkers of the
Middle Ages as Leonardo da Vinci's drawings are from the illu-
minations of missals. Yet Machiavelli is no isolated phenomenon
—from Salutati to Guicciardini, men were following the same
quest. What general rules can be derived from political experience? As history enshrines political experience, thinkers grew
profoundly interested in the past. In the Middle Ages political
philosophers were theologians, in the Renaissance they were historians. This change had been brought about by the conflict of
cities, the problems of despotism, and the crisis of liberty.

III

THE ARTS

In 1546 a young, successful painter, Giorgio Vasari, was at a small supper party in Cardinal Farnese's palace in Rome. The conversation turned to the extraordinary flowering of Italian art in the previous century and to the exceptional artists who had revolutionized painting and sculpture since the far-off days of Giotto and Pisano. Yet Vasari's presence was even more remarkable still, for even a hundred years earlier it would have been unthinkable for a young painter to have been a frequent guest at a cardinal's table. The social position of the artist had changed as much as art itself. To the men at that supper party, the age of heroes was passing; only the formidable genius of old Michelangelo could challenge, Vasari thought, the giants of the past. Encouraged and helped by the others, Vasari determined to collect all that men knew about these remarkable artists of the recent past; to immortalize, above all, the painters of Florence, which, for Vasari, was the cradle of the arts. Florence had nurtured what Rome had used. There had been a time when Milan, with Leonardo da Vinci at the court of Lodovico Sforza, had seemed about to be the leading city of the Renaissance. The great invasions cut that short. And it was Venice, secure and rich, that became the heir of Florence and the rival of Rome. Yet it was these four cities—Florence, Milan, Rome, and Venice—in which the practice and patronage of art had become a civic virtue; it was these cities that witnessed the triumphs of painting and sculpture and the emergence of the artist from the confines of a craft to the lonely pursuit of his genius.

In the early fifteenth century the artists had been as certain as Vasari that they were heralding a new age; behind them stretched dark and barren times. They acknowledged the genius of Giotto and Cimabue, but few others. Their admiration was kept for antiquity, which they yearned to equal, if not surpass, but certainly the modern age began with them: painting with Masaccio, sculpture with Ghiberti, architecture with Brunelleschi. And, indeed, this was not idle boasting. Donatello's statues possess exceptional originality. In painting the break is, perhaps, less vivid than in Donatello's free-standing statutes, but it is remarkable enough. In architecture success came more slowly. In literature and in music men were equally confident of their own originality and in the superiority of their age: between their own time and antiquity stretched the "barbarous Middle Ages." Soon against the broad sweep of modern history, their claims seem wholly justified. The language of Renaissance art is the language of the modern world—at least until recent times—whereas the art of the Middle Ages possesses some of the same difficulties as the art of Islam or India or China. Its beauty can be recognized, its contents discerned, but its impact on the feelings is never, or rarely, immediate.

And yet, as soon as one considers individual works of Renaissance art or considers the purpose for which they were painted or modeled or built, one is immediately aware how entangled the artists of fifteenth-century Italy were in the traditions not only of Gothic art but also of Byzantium. They were also deeply indebted to the imaginative originality and technical skill of the great Flemish and Burgundian school of painting and illumination. These strands of tradition and of foreign influence give an added richness of texture to the achievement of the Renaissance painters; but when all debts and obligations are acknowledged, what a fabulous achievement in painting and sculpture remains! Great artists are as common as peaks in the Himalayas, leading one to believe that the ability to draw or to carve is no rarer in human beings than mathematical skill and only requires the appropriate social circumstances to call it forth in abundance.

And certainly the social circumstances were exceptionally favorable for artists and craftsmen. Firstly there was a strong, deep-rooted tradition, which went back to the earliest days of Christian Europe, that men whom God had prospered should give thanks for their good fortune by embellishing the churches and monasteries in which He was worshiped. Building for God and the adornment of God's buildings were a part of the Christian life—sanctioned by time and anchored in belief. After all, it was the most vivid, the most dramatic way of reaching the illiterate. Therefore, it was inevitable that as the men of affairs flourished in Venice, in Florence, in Milan, or in Naples, they should wish their wealth to be reflected in their parish churches, in the monasteries and nunneries which they founded or patronized, and in the cathedrals of their cities. And in this exercise of artistic benevolence in the service of God, they had a supreme mentor in the Pope. At Avignon, and afterward at Rome, the popes had fostered a visual splendor that was the envy of the kings of Europe as well as the princes of Italy. The sense of merit in the visual expression of piety was universally held even by such naturally puritanical characters as Bernardino of Siena or Savonarola. Although they called for the burning of vanities, that did not include pictures of sacred subjects. To all men, even the most ascetic, these were a part of religion as old as the Church itself.

Furthermore, it had long been the custom of princes to adorn their palaces; to encourage the skilled crafts of metalwork and jewelry; to take delight in tapestries and frescoes that told them a well-loved story such as the Virgin and the Unicorn or reminded them of the pursuits—hunting or the art of love—in which they took delight. It satisfied their senses, as well as enhanced their pride, to read their prayers from costly books, illuminated with exquisite skill. By 1400, however, there were hundreds of merchants in Italy, and in Burgundy, who could afford the artistic elegance that had once been the prerogative of the country's aristocracy. And these merchants were city-born; often their families had risen to greatness with their towns, and their civic pride was as strong as chivalry, stronger perhaps than a knight's loyalty to his prince. And they wished their city to mirror their own greatness, to reflect in its buildings and their adornment the wealth in which they took such sturdy delight. The competitive state system of Renaissance Italy was not merely concerned with power; it flourished equally strongly in the arts. It added to the stature of kings to have a world-renowned artist attached to their courts; and the republics—particularly Florence and Venice—were as jealous of their geniuses as any king.

Into the pursuit of art, therefore, both money and social energy were poured, and the effect was as dramatic as the investment of capital during the nineteenth century in technology and invention—and in many ways similar in its results. Naturally, the need for artists drew some men into a career which they might otherwise have ignored. Any poor peasant boy who showed some natural skill was likely to find a sponsor among the neighboring gentry or local merchants, as did Mantegna, who had herded sheep in the fields near Padua until discovered by Squarcione. Of course, the greatest source was the families of craftsmen— the jewelers, goldsmiths, metalworkers, and decorative painters— in which there was a tradition of design and the opportunity for early apprenticeship. Yet probably only the religious life had before drawn its practitioners from such a wide social background or caught in its orbit such a rich variety of human temperament. And this in itself had a fertilizing effect on artistic expression.

To the competition for artists was added the competition by artists. In early centuries, the craftsman could spend a lifetime beautifying one cathedral or monastery, adding, perhaps, a personal variation to the traditional themes and colors in which he worked, but unconcerned with public reputation or rivalry with his fellow artists. By 1450 personal vendettas and public rivalry between artists had become a commonplace of Florentine and Venetian life, and again to the advantage of art, for they led men to attempt to exploit their techniques to the fullest, to give their imagination free rein, to emphasize the singularity of their personal vision. It needs the skilled eye of a connoisseur to distinguish between one Burgundian master of illumination and another; a child can tell the difference between a Botticelli and a Uccello. Of course, this does not mean that attribution is easy or absolute. A successful painter of the Renaissance was the head of a workshop—often, as with the Bellini or Tintoretto, a large-scale family affair in which brothers, sons, and even daughters joined. And, furthermore, apprentices abounded, and so did journeymen who were skilled in hands or costumes or backgrounds or *putti*. And, as ever, the works of the second-rate emulated slavishly the genius of a few.

The circumstances of the Renaissance encouraged the cultivation of individual style. And the rewards of the successful creation of a deeply personal idiom were so large that artists took risks which craftsmen in earlier days would never have dared take. Some men followed their daemons wherever they might lead, and painters committed themselves to their artistic vision with the fervor of a saint following his calling. The stories that Vasari tells may or may not be true, but they reveal what Italian society expected of the lives of its artists—Andrea del Castagno killing Domenico out of envy; Piero di Cosimo boiling the eggs that he lived on, fifty at a time, with his varnishes to save time; Paolo Uccello loving perspective so much more than his wife. What is common to all is the acceptance of dedication and the acceptance of self. This swarming crowd of painters, sculptors, goldsmiths, decorators, jewelers, contained men of widely differing gifts and most varied temperaments; men of profound curiosity such as Leonardo, of soaring imagination such as Michelangelo, of highly intellectual powers such as Piero della Francesca, of exquisite sensitivity such as Giorgione, and of supreme technical accomplishments such as Raphael.

The three great arts—painting, sculpture, architecture—changed most profoundly between 1400 and 1500. Indications that change might come had not been infrequent in the fourteenth century. Painting in the thirteenth century had been largely dominated by Greek (that is, Byzantine) influence—indeed, many of the artists were themselves Greek; the olive-skinned, slant-eyed, ikonlike madonnas of Cimabue and Duccio di Buoninsegna are refined expressions, with a hint of personal involvement, of established traditions. In comparison, Giotto towers like a giant, even if by fifteenth-century standards he is naïve and primitive. His figures have, to use Berenson's excellent phrase, "tactile values;" you feel that you could touch them, walk around them, and that they could walk around you. He used with great economy light, shade, color, and strongly featured men and women to give this sense of solid form and three-dimensional space. Yet for a hundred years there was little or no advance from his innovating skill, only imitation. Florentine art was, apart from Orcagna, less imaginative, less technically dexterous than the achievement of the great painters and illuminators of Burgundy, Flanders, and Avignon, whose skills were steadily to seep through the Alps to enrich Italy. Certainly Florence lacked the achievement of Siena, where strong Byzantine and weaker Gothic influences blended to create a school of painters—Lorenzetti, Martini, Duccio—of great charm and some originality, particularly in landscape.

Then, suddenly, as Italian art seemed to be drifting gently and skillfully into its own version of the Gothic, the promise of Giotto was fulfilled in one of the greatest of all Florentine painters—Masaccio. His frescoes in the Brancacci Chapel of the Carmine were revered by generations of artists, who subjected them to the closest study. His great abilities were not, however, like Giotto's, exercised in isolation. From 1400 onward two artists of outstanding ability—one a sculptor, Donatello, and

the other an architect, Brunelleschi—also helped to create a
totally new attitude to art. Both were entranced by perspective,
by human nature, and by reality as they saw it—not through
symbol or myth but directly and clear-sightedly. Donatello's
David was a piece of amazing originality; the beauty of a boy's
naked body displayed frankly for the first time since antiquity.
It marks as emphatically as Watt's invention of a modern steam
engine the birth of a new age. Brunelleschi contributed as
much, perhaps, by his ardent proselytism of the rules of perspective as by the soaring dome that he built for Florence's
cathedral. And in addition to these three others—Ghiberti,
Uccello, Luca della Robbia, Fra Angelico—painters and sculptors of exceptional talent, perhaps even touched with genius,
who were deeply moved by the new technical triumphs which
the study of perspective had brought; indeed, Uccello painted
with scarcely any other project in view than to demonstrate his
skill in handling perspective in the most unlikely circumstances.
Naturally, those men who in more recent times would have
turned to the career of a scientist or a mathematician were
deeply stirred by the complex harmonies that could be achieved
by following the strict rules of perspective. The greatest of these
was undoubtedly Piero della Francesca of Borgo San Sepolcro,
an artist of genius who in the end preferred his mathematics
to his art and painted nothing for the last fourteen years of his
life. He combined an exceptional control of linear relationships
with a sense of life that was both grave and serene. A preoccupation with, as it were, the density of things, combined
with a tragic view of life, became the dominant theme in
Florentine art. A further preoccupation was a sense of movement which infuses the reliefs, the statues, the pictures of this
extraordinary city, and was to culminate in the writhing nudes
of Michelangelo, locked forever in their struggle with Fate.
Power of intellect, gravity of feelings, a sense of Time, these
qualities artists were able to express visually.

Both Donatelo and Brunelleschi, who were devoted friends,

were concerned with other intellectual preoccupations apart from perspective. They searched deliberately and consciously for the antique. They went off together to Rome. Brunelleschi measured and drew ruin after ruin; Donatello studied the few Roman and fewer Greek bronzes and statues that men were beginning to collect at this time. And both men felt that they were the heirs of Rome, that between them and the fifth century there was a great gulf of barbarism.

And yet the art of the early fifteenth century was deeply entangled in its past. The scenes which painters were called upon to paint were the traditional scenes of Christian mythology—Nativities, Circumcisions, Crucifixions—the miracles of saints, the Stations of the Cross—and they were expected to execute them in traditional places, on the walls of churches and monasteries and on panels for altars. And skill in the control of perspective, or even a delight in the antique as absolute as Mantegna's, did not abolish the old symbols or the traditional iconography: four of five jagged rocks, realistically drawn, still represented mountains, as they had done for centuries in Byzantine art. The egg, hanging in the apse in Piero della Francesca's great picture of the Madonna and Child with saints, in the Brera, Milan, represents the four elements of the universe—a purely medieval symbol—as well as being a perfect conic section and the central point of a complex composition, requiring superlative skill in perspective. And although Uccello might gently mock the traditions of chivalry in his *Saint George and the Dragon,* nevertheless they absorbed his imagination; and Gozzoli's *Journey of the Magi* is as Gothic in feeling and intention as a fifteenth-century tapestry from Burgundy. Indeed, the new art of Donatello and Masaccio had no easy victory except in technique, for the Gothic feeling from the North seeped like an estuarine tide through the brushes and canvases of Italian artists of the fifteenth century: they were no more conscious of it than children playing with new toys in the sunshine, yet it caught them inexorably.

The other great triumphs of Renaissance art—the painting of landscape, the exploration of space and light through color, the full acceptance of the nude, and the development of the portrait —came only slowly.

And again they were partly due to foreign influence. Landscape in early Renaissance art was mainly the landscape of symbol, such as the paradisal gardens derived probably from Persia—containing sometimes delicately observed flowers and plants and animals, but painted for their value as symbols, not to stir feeling, not to evoke mood deliberately, except in a formalized and quasi-theological sense—or the terrible mountains, rocks, and forests which were the age-old symbols of hell and horror. But as individuality began to creep out from traditional expression, and as the control of technique became more certain, painters and illustrators could not resist the challenge of the outward-seeing eye. In the *Très Riches Heures* of the Duc de Berry, ordinary life is revealed—peasants cut the crops, the children swim, the sheep feed on the mountain side. About the time that these were being painted by the Limbourg brothers, a Flemish artist, Jan van Eyck, began to give small background landscapes to his great altarpieces, which influenced Italian art as profoundly as his discovery of oil painting. Both his feeling for landscape and his knowledge of oils were taken back to Italy, where Antonello da Messina was one of the first to employ the new technique. The exploration of color, of light and shade, of the intimate relation of man and nature, became dominant themes in Venetian art. Actually, Florentine artists had not been entirely indifferent to landscape; its study was partially involved in their preoccupation with perspective. Also, feeling inspired by natural objects was an integral part of their Neoplatonism. Brunelleschi made an optical device for viewing the city, and Alberti told how nature stirred him to tears and to joy. The intellectual problem of drawing figures against a distant background was bound to preoccupy Piero della Francesca, and he solved it about 1465, when he painted his great

Urbino diptych. And realistic landscapes, particularly of the Val d'Arno, were painted shortly afterwards by Pollaiuolo. But neither painter responded with such a deep sense of personal discovery as did Giovanni Bellini, although the stimulus for his preoccupation may have come as much from della Francesca as from van Eyck. Bellini loved light, loved the first clear light of morning that touches the mountaintops and leaves the plain in shadow, and the golden light of the last hours of day, the time that Leonardo was to love so deeply, a time that gives depth to shadow and softness and glow to color. Even the full light of midday in all its hardness and brilliance did not repel Bellini. He could drink in its heat and intensity, as his Saint Francis does with his outstretched arms, raised as much to the sun as to God. Although his delight in light and its effects on color passed into the Venetian tradition, his almost Brueghel-like concern with the detail of landscape did not.

Landscape was used by Giorgione, by Titian, by Tintoretto, to interpret mood, to reflect the emotion felt by the painter and to stimulate it in the beholder. In Giorgione and in the early works of Titian, landscape painting reached hallucinatory heights of feeling, reflecting mystery, horror, fear, tenderness, security, bliss, and love. As with perspective, so with landscape, a new world of artistic expression had been created.

The Venetians, of course, were not the only artists in the early sixteenth century to take delight in the painting of landscape. True, Michelangelo largely ignored it, and Botticelli used it merely as decoration or to emphasize his flowing, vibrant movement, but the Umbrian painters—Perugino and Pinturicchio—drew much from the tradition of Piero della Francesca; a tradition that was absorbed with masterful ease by Raphael. And, naturally, Leonardo da Vinci's sense of beauty as well as his avid curiosity were stirred by nature. The geological structure of mountains as well as their evocation of emotion caught his imagination, as did the turbulence of water as well as the mechanics of its flow; as did the flight of birds or the botany of flowers as well as their beauty; and, as in so many other aspects of Renaissance art, the scientific spirit and the delight in the eye were combined in one aesthetic pleasure, for in Leonardo the creative imagination was as multi-dimensional as geometry.

Throughout the Renaissance, artists were working for a small public. They were well known in their cities, they were familiar to popes and princes. The atmosphere in which they worked was intimate. Also, their art served a civic as well as a religious purpose. The Venetians realized early that narrative paintings about their heroic moments could have a public function, could impress both citizen and stranger with the republic's greatness. For the same reason, artists were paid to paint the vast pageants that gave drama and color and pomp to the Venetian year. In such pictures Venetians as well as Venice appeared, citizens as recognizable as the Piazzetta itself. The princes, too, helped to domesticate art. Their profiles had long adorned medals—indeed the only claim to fame of some of them is that Pisanello made a cast of their features. They hungered, as princes will, for eternity, and they needed not only to patronize painting or to construct huge palaces, but also to see themselves immortalized by one in order to adorn the other. They appeared, as the Medici did, in the retinue of kings making their offerings to the infant Christ, or in symbolic pageant, as Federico da Montefeltro and his wife, Battista, did in the Urbino diptych. And, of course, the preoccupation with the nature of man must of itself lead to the attempt to interpret character through portraiture; and for this the treatment of the face in profile was insufficient. Although there were brilliant portraits elsewhere —Pollaiuolo's *Portrait of a Man,* Botticelli's *Giovanni di Pierfrancesco de' Medici,* and many others—Venice was the true home of the portrait. A great series of doges, unhappily destroyed by fire in 1577, was painted by Bellini for the Doge's

Palace. And the portrait rapidly became fashionable. Procurators and merchants quickly followed in the steps of the doges, and the walls of private palaces were adorned with the portraits of their owners, many of them masterpieces of human interpretation by Titian.

Through perspective, through the introduction of oils, through the exploitation of landscape and the human body, Renaissance Italy created the traditions of Western art, in which it was to remain embedded for centuries. Sculpture and architecture had flourished in like manner. Donatello's *David* remained an isolated phenomenon only for a generation. Verrocchio, Leonardo, and, above all, Michelangelo created statues of a beauty that equaled the best that the ancient world had to offer, and Michelangelo infused his statues with an emotional force that none have equaled since. The tragic nature of man—his immense loneliness and his inevitable end—gripped him like a vise. His tension and suffering, generalized for mankind, passed into stone or paint. Social circumstance and technical change allowed such supreme artists to flourish. And the distance traveled in a little over a hundred years—from Lorenzo Monaco, Gentile da Fabriano, or Lorenzetti to Leonardo, Michelangelo, or Raphael—is stupendous. Such a leap was only possible because art had become the expression of complex social forces.

By the High Renaissance, art had come to pervade all aspects of life. From the arrangement of sweetmeats to the construction of fortifications—all were matters of moment upon which an artist's opinion might be needed or offered. And most of the great artists, too, regarded themselves as Jacks-of-all-trades. Leonardo did not think it beneath his dignity to design the costumes for the masques which his patrons loved or to fix the heating for a duchess' bath. And most of the great figures of the Renaissance displayed exceptional versatility. Michelangelo felt himself to be a man wholly dedicated to sculpture, yet after his reluctance had been overcome, he could paint the frescoes of the Sistine Chapel. And, of course, he could, and did, turn to architecture with equal facility and, when the mood was upon him, express his deepest feelings in poetry. The versatility of a Leonardo or a Michelangelo was far from being unusual. Princes and patrons wished their lives to be embellished richly, ostentatiously, beautifully, and they were willing to pour out their ducats and florins on all the arts and crafts that adorn the life of man. They pursued physical beauty like a drug. Their heightened sensibilities, due to the sudden turns of chance which threaded their days with light and shadow, lusted for color, richness, wanton display. This aristocratic spirit at large in a world of bourgeois delights had no use for pewter dishes, sober costume, modest feasting, or chaste jewelry. It reveled in gold, in silver, in bronze, in gaudy dishes of majolica, and in silks, in satins, and in damasks, in cunningly wrought pearls, in sapphires, in rubies, and in emeralds. And the pageantry, the masquerades, the feasts, the dancing, and the music provided the background to this peacock world. This pride, this ostentation could find expression in the intellectual world as well as in the senses, and collections of antique bronzes, marble statues, splendidly illuminated manuscripts, beautifully bound books from the new presses, ancient rings and seals, became a prince as much as his palace or his pictures. The mania for collecting, as a reflection of social grandeur, emerges during the Renaissance. This delight in the eye, this desire to impress, created a constant demand for the services of the great masters, even for the most trivial and most ephemeral commissions—the molding of pastry, the decoration of a table, the casting of a candlestick, the cutting of an intaglio, the design of a dagger—almost all of which have disappeared into limbo. The works of a few craftsmen of genius—the terracottas of della Robbia, the metalwork of Cellini, the bronzes of Riccio—survive. Those of nameless craftsmen who achieved high excellence are more plentiful. Their ornate *cassoni*, their haunting bronzes, their brightly patterned majolicas, and, above all, their exquisite jewelry, scattered about the museums of America and Western Europe, give a glimpse of the sumptuous world for which they worked.

This was the way, they thought, the great Romans had lived. They loved to act the parts of classical mythology, to be Jupiter or Hebe or Apollo or Diana for a day. And although, of course, they never gave up their Christian roots, they were drawn increasingly closer to the pretense of a pagan world. It gave them what all aristocracies need, a sense of separateness, as certainly and as completely as chivalry and feudalism had given a sense of caste to the warrior knights of the Middle Ages. Classical mythology, Neoplatonism, the mysteries of the pagan world, became fashionable. The education of a gentleman took on the strong classical bias which it was not to lose until modern times. The popular philosophers—Ficino, Pico della Mirandola, the friends of painters as well as their patrons—encouraged the revival of these ancient allegories. But they were not to be shared with the vulgar. Taste, sensibility, were to be linked with esoteric, almost private, knowledge. Poets, philosophers, painters, should speak in the language of riddles, of mysteries, which the *cognoscenti* alone could read. Such an attitude bred a sense of singularity, of exclusiveness, which courts and courtiers found as seductive as sin. Even Leonardo jotted down in commonplace books the trivial riddles of the Sforza, and Pico boasted in a philosophical essay, "If I am not mistaken it will be intelligible only to a few, for it is filled with many mysteries from the secret philosophies of the ancients." The esoteric, the mysterious, developed a fashionable cachet, and its cult opened the floodgates not only to much of the nonsense of late Neoplatonism, but also to astrology, to the language of emblems, and to the absurdities of late medieval bestiaries, and in the revival of learning there was intermingled a great deal of hocus-pocus. Much of this, however, is germane to the image that Renaissance man created of himself and will be dealt with later, but this delight in an exclusive world of myth and mystery also influenced artistic expression profoundly. A naked Mars and Venus, tired but happy from their wanton sport, might shock the uninitiated, but the cultivated knew better. Mars, of course, was War, and Venus Love, so Love could conquer War and bring forth Peace. And if by chance Venus was wearing a bit of the armor, that merely illustrated that Love itself involved Strife. Such were simple allegories which even the fringe of the elite could read, but the theology as well as the mythology of poetic virtue grew even more complex in its expression. Bellini's *Feast of the Gods* is the subject of a monograph, and all the iconographic scholarship of the Western world has failed to probe the hidden meanings of Giorgione's *Tempest*. For those artists who felt keenly the mystery of things, the way of allegory often proved enriching. It enabled them to explore feeling, to describe atmosphere, to hint at hidden presences, and to still in one luminous moment the fever and the fret of life and give its transience significance. So the *Virgin of the Rocks*, or even the *Mona Lisa*, possesses a sense of depth, of the abiding value of individual life, of eternal knowledge, that is both nostalgic and humane.

Giorgione responded to this sense of awareness as well as to Leonardo's mastery of light and shade. In Giorgione's paintings, and in many of Titian's, the value of earthly life is increased and given a significance that is as remote from the Middle Ages as it is from China.

A great artist like Giorgione could give universality to a private and exclusive myth, indeed deepen his genius by indulging in it, but many lesser artists could not. In their hands the mysteries became hollow, the allegories obvious and banal. Also, this cult of a private language of art marks the drift of the tide. The great masterpieces of the Renaissance had been, and many of them even in the first quarter of the sixteenth century still were, great public performances, even if they were created for popes or princes. But increasingly the direction of art was toward private enjoyment, and its style both more aristocratic and more exclusive. This was bound to be, as the heroic age of the city-state waned; as power and wealth and the sense of opportunity passed to the sea-borne nations of the West. Yet the achievement was so fabulously great that the traditions created in four or five generations proved far too strong for the creative imagination to wither quickly, and for the next four hundred years the arts of Italy continued to entrance the mind of Europe.

IV

FLORENCE
CRADLE OF HUMANISM

"In a few hours they were burnt, their legs and arms gradually dropping off; part of their bodies remaining hanging to the chains, quantity of stones were thrown to make them fall, as there was a fear of the people getting hold of them; and then the hangman and those whose business it was, hacked down the post and burnt it on the ground, bringing a lot of brushwood, and stirring the fire up over the dead bodies, so that the very least piece was consumed. Then they fetched carts, and accompanied by the mace-bearers, carried the last bit of dust to the Arno, by the Ponte Vecchio, in order that no remains should be found," wrote Landucci in his diary after watching the execution of Savonarola and his disciples. So ended the strange, doom-haunted Dominican monk from Ferrara, whose bitter tirades against luxury, greed, extortion, and tyranny had torn Florentine society apart.

The Piazza in which Savonarola met his end was adorned with some of the most profoundly moving works of Renaissance art. He had given the apocalyptic sermons for which he was condemned under the vaulting dome of the cathedral, itself a triumph of the new architecture. Among his audience had sat the flower of Italian humanism—Pico della Mirandola, Poliziano, and Marsilio Ficino, the president of the Platonic Academy—and he told them roughly that an old woman knew more of faith than their Plato. Even Lorenzo de' Medici, the greatest of all Florentine patrons, had sought his friendship, only to be spurned. Savonarola rejected the Renaissance. He would have none of it, ignoring the fact that for a hundred years Florence had led Italy in painting, in sculpture, in philosophy, in sophistication. Of all Italian cities, Florence had been the cradle of the Renaissance, but curiously, except in its very earliest days, the spirit of Savonarola had always been abroad. Florence was a city of violent contrasts, a city of the light and the dark.

Physically Florence deceives: the golden Tuscan landscape, so rich, so fertile, so gentle in climate, bespeaks a pastoral, idyllic, Virgilian life in which the rhythms of living achieve a harmony with nature. Here, if anywhere, is a countryside made for a Giorgione or a Titian, yet Florence produced neither, nor indeed any painter who sought to immortalize the poetry of nature. The facts of Florentine life were brutal, not gentle. Rich and beautiful its situation might be; economically and strategically its position was always desperate. To the west, controlling its only outlet to the sea, lay Pisa, prosperous and powerful, linked by its commerce with the four corners of the Mediterranean world. Athwart the route to Pisa, Florence had an unbeatable enemy in Lucca. To the north, the peril was worse—Milan, ravenous for land and rich in men and money. To the south, almost on Florence's doorstep, Siena controlled the road to Rome, and the Sienese were as fiercely proud and warlike as the Florentines. To the east were the wolves, the ravagers, the petty tyrants of the Papal Patrimony who lived by war and violence; for these despots the rich lands of Tuscany were sweet to plunder. To survive, therefore, let alone expand, Florence required from its citizens both courage and resourcefulness, a willingness to practice the arts of diplomacy as well as war. Both needed money, and, in the last analysis, wealth and wealth alone enabled Florence to survive and to triumph over the disadvantages of its geographical situation. The realities of Florentine life were the sword and the florin. The use of both was improved by skill in reading human nature, and it is not surprising that a preoccupation with man and his destiny lies at the heart of the Florentine Renaissance.

Despite all its perils, Florence triumphed. The prime source of its strength and wealth lay in its *arti*—the guilds which drew together its merchants and skilled craftsmen. One of the earliest to be organized was the *arte di Calimala,* and throughout the golden age of Florence it held its dominating position. It was a company of merchants who traded with England, Flanders, and France, bringing undressed cloths to Florence, where they were reworked into fine materials and dyed in the splendid, vivid colors that the Renaissance painters have made so memorable—the blues and crimsons and reds in which they dressed their saints and madonnas. They exported the finished goods throughout Europe, and the stamp of the guild became a guarantee of worth and workmanship. The guild was meticulously ruled and its members subjected to a close discipline not only in their public, but also in their moral life. The *Calimala* became a model for the other great guilds that began to dominate Florentine economic and political life in the late twelfth and early thirteenth centuries. Including the *Calimala* there were seven of them—the wool merchants, the silk weavers, the bankers, the notaries, the druggists (Dante was a member of this guild, which also dealt in spices and precious stones), and the furriers. These seven included all the great merchants of Florence, who formed the heart of its economic life. But Florence was a large town, and it served a populous hinterland, and its shopkeepers were numerous enough, and powerful enough, to form their own guilds, which were known as the lesser arts— the innkeepers, shoemakers, carpenters, blacksmiths, grocers, bakers, and the like—fourteen in all. Each guild had its officers of state—its consuls, its notaries, and its banner-bearer (*gonfaloniere*) who carried the heraldic symbols in the great proces-

sions which were held on the day of their patron saint. Each
guild, too, had its church which it patronized and in which
were held its special masses, for these merchants were as deeply
steeped in religion as in trade. (At the head of each page of
one of their surviving account books is the sign of the cross,
made to make forgery hell-worthy.) The Florentine guilds
were small worlds unto themselves, closely regulated, self-
conscious, jealous of their rights and customs, and fully aware
of their power.

Naturally, relations between the greater and lesser guilds
were often uneasy. The lesser guilds felt their numbers gave
them a right to power; the greater knew that, in the last resort,
it was their money which sustained the government of Florence both in peace and in war. Yet there were never more than
three or four thousand men in these twenty-one guilds, and
Florence embraced nearly a hundred thousand souls. The bulk
of the population was proletarian—workers for a day wage:
spinning, dyeing, weaving, carding, or hauling the great bales
of wool and cloth and silk—the citizens who, in the very beginning, had fought for the liberties within the city and for
its rich territories without, the people into whose hearts Savonarola's words burned like fire. They were organized into four
districts, each with four quarters led by a gonfalon—the Unicorn, the Viper, the Lion—under which each citizen was en-
rolled to fight, if need be, for his city's liberty. From these
quarters were drawn the governors of the city who made up
the Signory which ruled Florence, made peace or war, and
levied the taxes. Naturally, the Signory was attended with immense ceremonial and its chief officers, the priors, lived in
grandeur, but their tenure was as brief as a butterfly's for they
ruled for two months only. To control this complex govern-
mental machine, men fought in the streets, assassinated, exiled,
pillaged, and destroyed each other generation after generation,
so that one Florentine gloomily remarked that there were

enough citizens in exile to populate another city. The main strife revolved about who should or who should not be prior-worthy—whether, in fact, power should be widely distributed or kept close—and whether the major arts or the minor arts should dominate the institutions of government. There was factional strife not only within the ranks of the guilds but among the restless proletariat, often made politically conscious by the hunger of their bellies, for Florence suffered the sharp economic storms of an uncontrolled capitalism. So over the centuries power in Florence swayed like sea-weed in a tide, drifting into the hands of oligarchs only to be snatched out, but never for long, by a great upsurging wave of popular feeling.

During most of the Renaissance, political power in Florence was in the hands of a group of very rich merchants, led by the Medici family. This closely knit oligarchy controlled all the elections to office with the sureness of a Tammany machine. Better still for them, they handled the city's taxes. And, of course, they were the inheritors of the vast wealth which the far-flung trade of Florence had drawn from the four quarters of Europe.

Suspicious, guarded, rich, the oligarchs clung tenaciously to their power, willing to serve the Medici only as long as the Medici served them. Their greed and envy occasionally drew them close to conspiracy, and the plot of the Pazzi family to kill the Medici in the Duomo toppled some of them into disastrous treason. Politically and financially these men had lit-tle foresight: they exploited their power to siphon the city's riches into their own pockets. Yet they had one saving grace: they had been born into a tradition of civic patronage. Their fathers, and their fathers before them, had endowed monasteries, beautiful churches, and established charities. A sense of sin still clung to usury and to the banker's trade, and they had felt a need to return a tithe of their profits. Naturally, they were stirred by particular acts of God's goodness to them, and then their piety turned more quickly into patronage. Yet about 1400 this tradition began to change, both in its nature and its expression.

This change was wrought by a desperate war, working on the literary and artistic movements which had already seeded themselves in Florence, and the result was a remarkable leap forward in painting, in sculpture, in architecture, in philosophy, and in the countless arts and crafts that adorn the life of man. The change was as dramatic as water turning into ice.

After its failure by 1343 to secure dominion of Tuscany by force of arms, Florence had resolved to ally, whenever possible, with neighboring city-states, to protect rather than absorb. As Coluccio Salutati, the chancellor of Florence and one of its first great humanists, wrote, the Florentines who hated tyranny at home were willing to defend the liberties of others. The feeling was strong in the city's governing circles that Florentines were the true heirs of republican Rome: Salutati, Bruni, and Poggio studied Cicero in their leisure from running Florence's diplomacy and collecting its taxes. His ideas, which lie at the heart of humanism, struck them with the force of a new discovery, and they began to weave afresh the belief that the full life, indeed, the good life, could ónly be lived if a man dedicated himself to civic virtues. It was about Rome, about Cicero, about Plato, that they talked when they lingered in the sun in the Piazza or gathered together in each other's houses. Nor did they disdain to discuss their ideas with the sculptors and artists—Ghiberti, Donatello, Brunelleschi—whom they and their friends patronized. And how right they seemed in their interpretation of the past and the present, when Florence withstood alone the might of Gian Galeazzo Visconti, who, in 1402, stood poised to overwhelm the city and so bring the whole of Lombardy and Tuscany under his sway. Then, as in some Athenian tragedy, the Fates took up their shears. Gian Galeazzo, in the prime of life, with the cup of success at his lips, sickened and died. So the threat to Florence passed, but, in passing, fused a mood into an attitude to life.

The Florentines did not consider themselves saved by chance. For them it was a triumph of civic virtue, of steadfast republicans thwarting tyrants. The ancient Roman virtues of which Cicero spoke and of which old Cato was the ideal, had been, they felt, reborn in Florence, which gave the city an identity with the past. The year 1402 represented a triumph and a liberation, and this sense of freedom renewed, of the breaking of the shackles of the immediate past, invigorated not only philosophy and history but also the plastic arts. It is not surprising that Masaccio's grave saints should wear their cloaks like togas.

Interest in classics, interest in ancient art, delight in new techniques of painting, sculpture, and architecture, existed before the cataclysmic struggle with Milan, but none can doubt that it gave an immense impetus to the peculiar qualities of the Florentine Renaissance. Symbolically, at the height of the struggle the city appointed Chrysoloras, the first and most deeply influntial teacher of Greek, a public lecturer. A belief in the value of classical learnings as the molder of a citizen's character, a conviction that great moral value could be derived from a study of its philosophy, became as deeply embedded in the Florentine tradition as it did in nineteenth-century England. And when the Medici founded and encouraged a Platonic academy, and patronized handsomely the great philosophers—Ficino, Pico, and the rest—they were no innovators, and the purpose of their patronage was widely understood. It would strengthen an attitude to human life that was thought to be singularly Florentine. Although humanistic study had its roots in civic life, naturally it developed rapidly within the terms of its own disciplines and needs. Scholars dedicated themselves to the textual and philological problems inherent in the study of the classics—and as scholars will, became obsessed with their own techniques. Yet even if preoccupation with style, grammar, emendation, and the minutiae of criticism often took the place of creative imagination, there was nevertheless a great deal of fine poetry and fine prose, written in a Latin that would have been no disgrace to the age of Augustus. And the encouragement to classical studies given by the humanistic Renaissance in Florence was in harmony with scholarly activity scattered throughout the courts and cities of Italy.

Yet the greatest gains from this self-identification with the antique were in the arts, particularly sculpture. As in ancient Athens, statues taught citizens the lessons of their public life. The mysterious David of Donatello and the vast David of Michelangelo both told the Florentines that their city had always been a giant-killer, proud of its liberty: the citizens themselves dragged the statue of Holofernes and Judith from the Medici palace and set it up in front of the Palazzo della Signoria to underline what should be the fate of tyrants. In no other place were sculptors so handsomely patronized or so deeply admired. Florence, in consequence, produced the greatest masters of the fifteenth century, whose work graced Rome, Venice, Milan, and the lessers cities of Italy. So, too, in architecture: while Milan and Venice still lingered in the grip of the Gothic, and Rome lay in ruins, Brunelleschi began recreating the austere harmonies of the classical world and giving to the Florentines a proper setting for their intense civic consciousness. In painting there was the same sense of *gravitas,* of weight of human character, of the power of human destiny, particularly before the sophistication and self-indulgence of the High Renaissance produced in some artists a more esoteric cultivation of art. Even so, the last great artist of Florence, Michelangelo, still recalls the tradition of his city, created by Giotto and Masaccio.

The struggle with Milan did more than render humanism fashionable, or encouraged a cult of the antique, or stimulate the arts, or make a study of Cicero an essential part of the education of a gentleman. It consolidated the power of the oligarchy, and peculiarly so, as the lucky death of Gian Galeazzo not only plucked them from the jaws of destruction, but set them on a course of military success. Surging economic prosperity was linked with the triumph of their arms. Florence, still free, still republican, enjoyed a prosperity, a fame, a serenity unparalleled in her annals—giving further point, if point were needed, to the antique virtue of her government and its citizens. Oligarchies, however, are rarely stable for long; after the first difficulties, criticism is quickly followed by intrigue. The death in 1417 of Maso degli Albizzi, the most powerful member of the ruling oligarchy, unleashed a struggle for power in which the old class and guild antagonisms once more erupted to the surface. By dexterous exploitation of these jealousies, Giovanni de' Medici and, after his death in 1429, his son Cosimo were able to establish their family so securely in power that Cosimo's grandson Lorenzo enjoyed the power if not the title of a prince. Yet even at the height of the family's greatness, respect was always paid to the letter of the republican constitution. The survival of the Medici and the ease with which they defeated the conspiracies of the Neroni and, afterward, of the Pazzi, were due to the loyal support of their fellow merchants as well as their dependents.

During this half-century of Medicean rule, Florence dominated the intellectual and artistic life of Italy: Cosimo poured out a torrent of wealth on buildings—palaces, monasteries, churches —on sculpture, and on paintings. Feeling himself to be God's debtor, he did his best to make restitution—reconstructing and embellishing his favorite monastery of San Marco, as well as his parish church of San Lorenzo. Following in his footsteps, his son Piero ordered a sumptuous tabernacle for the miraculous crucifix in San Miniato al Monte, and another for the wonder-working image at Santissima Annunziata, which bears the proud boast that the marble alone cost four thousand florins. Cosimo built his own palace modestly but strictly according to the new style; he patronized Donatello for as long as he lived, and sculpture, as might be expected from so dedicated a Florentine, was his greatest passion after architecture. He preferred his sons to deal with mere painters and decorators, but *he* paid. And many superb frescoes of Fra Angelico, Filippo Lippi, and Benozzo Gozzoli were the fruits of Medicean gold, of their sense of the usurer's sin, of a need to return the riches that one man had acquired in beauty that all could enjoy.

Lorenzo the Magnificent, his grandson, amazed by the staggering sums that his grandfather had spent, preferred the cheaper patronage of philosophers. Nevertheless, he maintained the tradition of his ancestors, and the beauty and splendor of Florence steadily grew. The citizens were continuously regaled with pageants, tournaments, and carnivals. It proved to be a reckless world in which capital was too easily squandered on military maneuvers, diplomatic activity, and Lorenzo's anxiety to cut a figure in Italy whatever the cost.

As the fame of Florence reached new heights, so did its public debt (not that the debt worried the oligarchy overmuch, for they lent the money on excellent security and at a splendid interest). The world was a rich man's oyster: the tentacles of Florentine trade stretched from Cairo to the Cotswolds, and even the shocks and disasters in the eastern Mediterranean— the spread of the Ottoman Turks and the fall of Constantinople —seemed, for a time at least, to be turned to Florence's advantage by a benign Providence. The loss of Byzantine alum, so vital to the luxury cloth trade, was immediately countered by the discovery of huge deposits at Tolfa in the Papal States, for which, naturally, the Medici secured the concession. Wandering Greeks with manuscripts to sell and an ancient tongue to teach were welcomed as a further adornment to a refined household. Secure and self-indulgent, the leaders of Florentine society tried

to evade present disasters and future cataclysms, while the
Florentine government sought to survive by the use of mercenaries, diplomacy, subsidies, and bribes. The call to civic
virtue, the mobilization of the city's wealth and the city's men,
no longer appealed to a bourgeois aristocracy. Their exclusive
world possessed too much delight to be foolishly risked. In the
soft elegance of Lorenzo di Pierfrancesco de' Medici's villa, in
the golden glow of the Tuscan evening, young men might listen
to Ficino's subtle explanations of the hidden meanings in Botticelli's *Primavera,* which adorned its walls; for them the bales
of wool, rolls of cloth, stacked hides, and piled spices were a
necessity, not a way of life, and although they could use the
dagger and the sword, they felt no compulsion to sweat in
arms amid the horrors of war for the future of their city. All
the authority, all the skill, of Lorenzo were used to avoid such
bleak necessities. This elegant world was perched precariously,
however, on the edge of turbulence, and it depended on the
subtlety and statesmanship of Lorenzo not only to prevent the
system from collapsing in internecine strife, of which the Pazzi
conspiracy was a clear enough warning, but also still the dangerous antipathy of a restless population whose fears and hopes
were already being played upon by a master demagogue, some
years before Lorenzo's death.

The Florentine Renaissance has entranced generations of men
by the astonishing range of its artistic and scholarly achievements—from the serene perfection of Leonardo to the tragic
realism of Machiavelli—and all too often the endless toil of
the laboring men and women, whose grievous lives made it
possible, is forgotten. It was the tragic situation of the common
man that stirred deeply the creative imagination not only of
Michelangelo, but also of Botticelli, who reflected the bright
elegance and exclusive charm of the Florentine world more
faithfully than any other painter. The compulsive rantings of
Savonarola haunted them both.

The last decades of the fifteenth century brought a sharp contraction of Florentine trade. Englishmen were beginning to make their own cloth, the Flemish were showing a more than Italian skill in dressing and dyeing it. In 1478 the London bank of the Medici was closed; in 1483 the Tolfa alum concession had to be abandoned; for a time the merchants of Florence even lost their traditional role as papal bankers. Trade with the eastern Mediterranean steadily wasted away. Renewed wars, with expensive alliances and even more costly condottieri, added further strain to an economy which had already accumulated far too many obligations. The Florentines had been dealing in futures for too many generations, and, skillful as their financiers were, they could not conjure increased wealth from diminishing trade. For centuries urban poverty had helped to breed epidemic diseases that raged with the ferocity of a prairie fire through the dirt-encrusted slums. Plagues, fevers, and consumption made death a constant visitor at the houses of the poor, who, to exorcise horror, fortify their courage, and set their hopes on future blessedness, pleaded for the intercession of the Virgin and the saints. Religion—ecstatic, even apocalyptic —assuaged the wounds of their poverty and its pain. For them the elegant, exclusive domain of the scarlet-wearing burghers who exercised authority in their city was a bright, elusive world as impossible to understand as dreams in a language they could never comprehend. The sufferings of Christ and the pity of God lay closer to their knowledge, and in their lives the priest was as necessary as bread. This contradiction—poverty, suffering, and pain amid a world of profusion, extravagance, and delight—stirred the consciences of deeply sensitive men. It was this that made Pico della Mirandola seek the solace of Savonarola's mysticism, that led him, at his death, to adopt the habit of a Dominican; it was this that brought about that stranger conversion which drew Botticelli away from the gaieties and urbane moralities of the antique to an acceptance of Savonarola's prophecies; it was this that fused Michelangelo's tragic sense of human destiny with Savonarola's apocalyptic vision.

The story of Savonarola is a mixture of tragedy and hysteria, in which a genuine pity for man's condition became enraveled in hate and muddled by political intrigue. His denunciation of worldliness, his childish burning of vanities, his fiery condemnation of a lazy and corrupt clergy, were a part of the threnody of the life of Europe, frequently heard, frequently forgotten; but Savonarola spoke at a time when the young Piero de' Medici was displaying a singular lack of his family's genius. Behind Savonarola loomed the discontented poor, eager for a change, eager for secular as well as religious hope. Those families whom the Medici had excluded and despised knew how to manipulate this superlative demagogue, whose wild sermons could inflame a multitude. So what started in evangelism finished in political revolution.

The little people, the *piagnoni* (snivelers) as the old oligarchs called them, became a power in the land. *Popolo e Libertà* frequently echoed in the Piazza—a cry which Pisa promptly adopted as it threw aside the Florentine yoke and claimed the protection of the French, when invasion of Italy had triggered the revolution against Piero. Savonarola combined a dependence on the French that was quite unrealistic with a hatred of the Papacy that bordered on insanity. His loud denunciations of papal sins (interlarded from time to time with staggeringly sane bits of hardheaded diplomacy) grew more shrill as the French left him in the lurch. Alexander VI—aware of, and tolerantly amused by, his own shortcomings—bore with the fulminations so long as his diplomacy required it. Time, of course, favored the Pope. The French were content to use Florence, but naturally disinclined to save it from the consequences of its own folly, or to restore its Tuscan empire. And in Florence itself, the oligarchs disliked both the rantings of Savonarola and the government of the people; in the wings lurked the exiled Medici—*they* were powerful in Rome. The inevitable end came: the rack and the fagot for Savonarola; the defeat of his *piagnoni*; and in the fullness of time, the return of the Medici.

The whole Savonarola episode is a curious mixture of idealism, ineptitude, and iniquity. Certainly Savonarola wanted a Florentine government that represented more fully the whole citizenship—the poor and the dispossessed as well as the rich and the powerful. He also hated life, grew drunk on his own megalomaniac visions, preferred prophecy to policy, and welcomed the disasters he had done so much to promote. Ignorance married to prejudice, blind hatred linked with a disgust for life, proved an unsatisfactory basis for statesmanship, even practiced by a saint.

Never again was the republic the same; the power of Florence was greatly diminished. For a decade after the burning of Savonarola in 1498 for heresy, and after the failure of her mercenaries, Florence's blood and treasure were poured out in the Pisan war. In 1509 Pisa was captured, but the expense was far beyond the weakened resources of Florence's dwindling trade. Indeed, three years later a refusal to act in concert with the Papacy was treated by Julius II as an impertinence. His professional Spanish troops scattered the Florentine militia. The papal-inspired revolution followed, and the Medici returned. They lacked the ability of their ancestors, and proved little better than pawns in the hands of the Medici Pope Leo X, and it required further rebellions and plots, another brief republic haunted by the puritanism and religiosity of Savonarola, as well as the sack of Rome by Charles V, before Florence was finally subjected to the rule of the Medici as dukes of Tuscany. In the first three decades of the sixteenth century the greatness of Florence faded. Economically—and the splendor of the Florentine Renaissance was based on its wealth—Florence lacked a future. The heart of its trade—cloth—was lost to England and to Flanders, and banking followed trade. Florence was far more vulnerable than Venice, or even Milan, to the great decline in Mediterranean prosperity which followed the discoveries of the New World and the sea-route to the Indies.

Artists lived uneasy lives in post-Medicean Florence, for patronage grew scarce. Art and humanism no longer reflected the civic virtues—these were adequately exercised by private prayer and public repentance. During the middle decades of the sixteenth century, the cult of sensitivity, of elegance, and of learning as the peculiar attributes of a gentleman had also narrowed the social basis of art and, to some extent, limited its appeal. In the wanderings of Leonardo and of Michelangelo, in the frustrations that marred their lives and marked their art, there is a reflection of the growing impotence and decay of the society in which they were born and grew to manhood.

Yet that tradition of individual destiny, of the worth of man, which the Florentines had cultivated so carefully in their heroic days, remained strong enough not only to sustain them in spite of the tribulations of their age, but also to buoy up a number of artists of lesser genius—Bronzino, Pontormo, del Sarto, and Fra Bartolommeo. And to one art, namely history, the decay of Florence provided a greater stimulus than its climb to greatness. The cataclysms of Florentine experience opened the same creative vistas for Machiavelli and Guicciardini as neuroses in individuals were to do for Dostoevsky or Proust. Indeed, even in its last, sad days, republican Florence still produced an astonishing array of genius, and no city of so small a compass has ever before, or since, made a greater contribution to art and letters within the brief span of a hundred and fifty years.

V

MILAN

CITY OF STRIFE

Milan seemed singularly favored by nature; to the south, over an easy pass in the Apennines, lay the great seaport of Genoa, a city of such majesty that the Venetians feared its power and envied its wealth; to the west and north swept the great arc of the Alps, as natural a frontier as a statesman could wish for; the few mountain passes that led to France or southern Germany gave Milan control of the routes from the great Genoese emporium to the markets of the North. Seen spread across an atlas of physical geography, the great, fertile valley of the Po seems one of the more natural places in Europe for the development of a strong unified state. Between the fall of the Roman Empire and the unification of Italy in the nineteenth century this was achieved only once—by Napoleon. The history of the Lombard plain is a history of invasion and war. For more than a thousand years some of Europe's bloodiest battles were fought on it. If Florence belonged to Minerva, Milan belonged to Mars.

The trouble lay partly in the fertily of the alluvial plain: the great walls of the Alps and the Apennines gave it some of the forcing quality of a hothouse. Crops grew with ease; heavy crops meant a large and prosperous population; and the whole of Lombardy was studded with thriving cities—Turin, Pavia, Lodi, Brescia, Bergamo, Vicenza, Verona, Padua, Ferrara, Bologna, Mantua, Parma, Piacenza, and Alessandria, among others. Only in times of desperation were these cities capable of acting in unity, as when the Emperor Frederick Barbarossa attempted to extend his power over them; otherwise they were content to intrigue and plot and fight among themselves. From time to time a city or a family arose like a bubble in this boiling cauldron, and like a bubble burst. Furthermore, the Holy Roman Emperor often found it advantageous to strengthen his natural aristocratic allies at the expense of the communes, for the Emperor preserved the legal right of overlordship, even if he failed often enough to exercise it in fact. What he never failed to do, once he possessed the strength, was to angle for greater power in these troubled but fish-laden waters. In this he was not alone. The princes of Savoy found morsels of the Lombard plain far sweeter than the granite wastes of the Alps which their country bestrode. Beyond Savoy were the French, whose king was willing to try to hold Savoy in check—at a price—or urge him forward if they were unpaid. And naturally the two great parties, the Guelphs and the Ghibellines, which polarized so many ancient feuds, thought that they could manipulate the great European powers to their advantage.

Milan and its satellite cities had failed to do what Florence and the Tuscan towns had succeeded in doing—they had never subjected the feudal nobility to the authority of the merchant class. In this bull ring of Europe, it is not surprising that men harassed by invasion, ruined by petty strife, and hamstrung by vendettas should dream of a "natural" state in which princes —powerful, all-wise, and intensely patriotic—should succeed generation after generation, wielding an iron authority that brought peace and fame. At times the imagination of poet and panegyrist soared in a wilder flight and saw the princes of Milan, whether Visconti or Sforza, adding to the duchy of Lombardy the kingship of all Italy. There were three dukes of Milan—Gian Galeazzo Visconti, Francesco Sforza, and Lodovico Il Moro—who, for the brief periods of their rule, removed, at least, all absurdity from this vision, although they were far too realistic ever to indulge themselves in such fantasies. Nevertheless, they did between them what no other rulers did: they created a state equal in power and wealth to Florence and to Venice. Milan, which became the epitome of the Renaissance state, is best seen reflected in the lives of its three greatest dukes.

The Visconti's emblem was a viper, and they had needed all the serpent's cunning not only to survive the vicissitudes of a fickle and bloody fortune but also to grow in riches and in authority. By the time Gian Galeazzo Visconti was born in 1351, his family had played a leading part in Lombardic affairs for over two hundred years. They had resolutely defended the interests of the merchants, acquired increasing judicial authority from the Holy Roman Emperor to provide a legal basis for their power, and arranged their marriages with dynastic prudence. Nevertheless, his father had been forced to fight for his inheritance, for the death of a Visconti ruler, followed as it was by the division of his lands among his heirs, always provided an opening to rebels and exiles in the discontented cities on the fringes of their lands. Galeazzo II shared the Visconti territories with his brother Bernabò, who ruled in Milan, while he remained at Pavia. Bernabò struggled to regain Bologna, Galeazzo to push westward to the Alps; in so doing they aroused a hornets' nest, and in 1373 they were nearly overwhelmed. It was a typical story of treachery, turbulence, and violence that fed the darker side of Galeazzo's nature—his suspicion, his avarice, his hate. His son Gian Galeazzo, born of his diplomatic marriage with Blanche of Savoy, was turned as quickly as possible to dynastic ends. At the age of nine he was married off to Isabelle of Valois, a princess of France, and by the time he was fourteen she had produced him a son. Both in battle and in diplomacy he proved equally precocious; but when he inherited his father's lands in 1378, his position was far from enviable. His uncle Bernabò, with a reputation for brutality and violence even in his own age, still ruled in Milan, and he had five sons, all ambitious, all land-hungry.

Gian Galeazzo was already known for his resource and cunning, but the latter got the better of his discretion. He suddenly made a wild bid for greatness. He secretly negotiated his own betrothal (his first wife had died at twenty-three) to the heiress of Sicily—a bargain that stood if he consummated the marriage within twelve months. The news outraged the particularist sentiments of the Italian princes, and they made certain that the bride never got within five hundred miles of her groom. And while Gian Galeazzo was wrestling with his strange problem of logistics, his uncle Bernabò extorted concession after concession from him, to make certain that the Visconti of Pavia should never be linked with the power of Sicily to the discomfiture of the Visconti of Milan. When the year had passed, Gian Galeazzo found himself without a wife and tied dynastically far tighter than he had ever been to his uncle, for the latter insisted that, having failed with the heiress of Sicily, Gian Galeazzo's bride should be his daughter Caterina, and no obstruction was placed before the immediate consummation of this marriage.

Gian Galeazzo complied, and brooded. He cultivated his garden. He devoted his considerable intelligence and remarkable concentration to the problems of government. He reduced taxation, reformed administration, weeded out corruption, and what leisure he had from the cares of government he spent on the adornment of his palace, the conversation of scholars, and consultation with astrologers. Although he enjoyed a reputation for piety, he placed his trust in the efficacy of the zodiac rather than of prayer, and when the stars were truly propitious, he set out on a pilgrimage to the Madonna del Monte at Varese. His timidity was known, and his entourage therefore surprised no one by its size; he hesitated (it was assumed through fear) to enter Milan, so his uncle and his cousins rode out to meet him. After an affectionate greeting they were taken prisoner, and Gian Galeazzo entered Milan to cries of "Long live the Count, and down with the taxes!" Gian Galeazzo's wife seems to have taken the destruction of her father and brothers with the phlegm usual in a Renaissance princess. The boldness of his enterprise was widely admired, and even Geoffrey Chaucer in far-off London turned a few verses on the event in his *Canterbury Tales*.

This success naturally gave Gian Galeazzo confidence, and since he was highly intelligent, he learned from it. More important than the timing of the plot, in the proper conjunction of the stars, was the fact that the Milanese did not close their gates but welcomed him as a liberator—a sentiment which he quickly turned to an article of faith by distributing some of Bernabò's treasure to the great financial relief of those whom he needed as allies. For the next seventeen years he exploited the paternalism of his government so that he might realize his almost insatiable dynastic ambitions. In order to impose his iron despotism, he posed as the liberator of cities and men. His success was the result of unwearying application, aided by good fortune and blended with a nice sense of contingencies. "He was wont," wrote his chronicler, Giovio, "to give himself up to meditation during solitary walks, to hold discussions with those who were most experienced in every branch of affairs, to quote instances from the annals of the past. He found relaxation for his mind in the conversation of scholars and in constant reading." Not for him, it would seem, "the delights of hunting or hawking, nor games of dice, nor the allurements of women, nor the tales of buffoons and jesters." He thought, he planned, he acted. In two swift campaigns, having made certain that treachery was rife in the cities he wished to conquer, he had absorbed all of eastern Lombardy save Mantua and Ferrara.

The Florentines, of course, were deeply disturbed to see one tyrant control all the Alpine passes on which so much of their trade depended, and they used their powers of persuasion, of which the florin proved the most efficacious, to raise a league against Gian Galeazzo. This merely succeeded in enlarging Gian Galeazzo's ambitions, for he was quick to realize that his gains could never be consolidated so long as Florence remained unsubjected. To do this he proceeded with skill and caution; each city-state had its party that hated Florence or the powers that ruled it. He fought wars when he had to, but he adroitly avoided a head-on collision with the combined powers of Florence and Venice. By 1402 he had acquired control of Pisa, Siena, Perugia, and Bologna, and it was within his power to strangle Florence politically and economically. The foundation of a great northern Italian kingdom seemed within his grasp, when he caught a fever and died.

By that time Gian Galeazzo had done more than enlarge the boundaries of his dukedom, for he had created a state as well as a despotism. He centralized government, reformed administration, and removed inequalities and special rights and privileges. Where possible he weakened the feudal nobility and encouraged the merchant class. He tried to fulfill the ideal which his humanists at Pavia had delineated—that of a "natural prince" whose state was serenely based on justice and equality. And by these means he had created the duchy of Milan, a coherent state that was to last until Napoleon swept it away. In many ways he is the prototype of the Rennaissance prince—unscrupulous in diplomacy, yet deeply concerned for the welfare of the state; passionately ambitious for his dynasty, yet aware of the needs of his country; scholarly, remote, and dedicated to the pursuit of power.

Gian Galeazzo's death broke up his empire. His captains of war thought no opportunity better for taking their pickings; the Tuscan and Umbrian cities, mindful now of the power of Florence, threw off their allegiance. The Venetians' indifference to Gian Galeazzo's success turned to alarm; his demise brought about a fundamental change in their policy. They decided to be a Lombard power—to secure territorial control of the Alpine passes which they needed for their trade, and of sufficient territory to give them ground for maneuver against a resurgent Milan. Once again the great feudal families whose power Gian Galeazzo had attempted to reduce flourished their standards. The Colleoni, Anguisola, Cavalcabò, and Correggio demanded their pounds of flesh, and the plain of Lombardy once more reeked of blood and slaughter, pillage and rape. In the midst of this desolation the Milanese core of the Visconti state held firm. It is a measure of Gian Galeazzo's success that it did so, for in some ways his heir was a greater disaster than the conflagrations of war that consumed Lombardy. Although it is certainly untrue that he fed his hounds on human flesh, such were his tyrannies that the Milanese had no difficulty in believing the story. His assassination in church in 1412 caused no surprise. Perhaps as a tribute to his brother's memory, his successor, Filippo Maria, had the murderers put to death by the most refined tortures. By nature Filippo Maria was not excessively cruel, merely neurotic. He was obese to the point of ridicule, and ugly to the point of embarrassment. His portrait was never painted, his marriage never consummated, and his appearance in public rare. Nevertheless, he ruled with skill if without panache. He maintained the machinery of the state and kept his head above the turbulent waters of Italian politics. Precluded by nature from the pursuit of martial glory, he was content to employ one of the best condottieri for this duty— Francesco Sforza—at least from time to time, for Filippo could never trust anyone for long.

Sforza, the son of one of the first great Italian condottieri —Muzio Sforza—came, as most condottieri did, from the Romagna, which had little to sell but the strength of its men. Sforza proved himself a great captain. His direct manner, tough physique, and aggressive nature made him an excellent general; his attention to detail, ferocious discipline, and deep personal loyalty gave him a band of soldiers of passionate devotion and exemplary technique. His personal magnetism was such that he won the enduring friendship of the two most outstanding men of his day—the highly sophisticated and cultivated banker Cosimo de' Medici, and the equally highly cultivated condottiere Federigo da Montefeltro. In the hard, tough school of war he won himself a vast reputation and a small territory, too small either for his purse or his ambition. And the situation in Milan was as clear to him as to his friends. Cosimo de' Medici did not relish the steady advance of Venetian power across the Lombard plain (the Alpine passes were vital to Florentine trade, and the Venetians were traders first and republicans second). A powerful, friendly Milan had become a necessity to Florence, so Cosimo provided Francesco with good advice and handsome loans. Federigo, as generous a condottiere as ever lived, admired Francesco's prowess as only a professional could, but he preferred, naturally enough, that Francesco should win his kingdom in Lombardy and not on *his* doorstep in the Romagna, where the Sforza had their patrimony.

Filippo Maria did not need to be instructed in the drift of their thoughts, for he was as subtle as his father if less ambitious. It proved toil enough for him to weld together the Visconti lands, bring the recalcitrant nobles and cities to a proper subjection, and withstand the encroachments of Venice. For these projects he needed Francesco, and to stay alive for his natural span in his castle of Milan, it was necessary to keep Sforza both expectant and dependent. So Francesco rattled his sword, and Filippo Maria dangled his daughter—not a legitimate daughter, of course, but a mistress had been more skillful than a wife, and Bianca was the result. The long wrangle ended in a betrothal; a longer engagement ended in a wedding; the wedding ended in a son and heir. Before, however, his succession had been determined, Filippo died, when Francesco was away from Visconti territory.

The Milanese erupted with republican sentiment, abolished

the dukedom, and created chaos. Neither Venice nor Florence
was amused by the advent of a sister republic and gave no help
as its troubles multiplied. Sforza moved cautiously until the
republic crumbled, and when he finally entered Milan, the citizens went wild with delight, rushed him and his horse into the
Duomo, and acclaimed him duke. For many years that was the
sole right the Sforza had to their dukedom—that and the sharp
edge of their swords—for the emperors refused to acknowledge
them. The powers of Italy, however, lacked the prejudice of
the Germans, and while Francesco consolidated his power with
military precision, the Medici got a bank in Milan, and alliances were formed with France, Savoy, Naples, and Florence.
The Sforza went bullheaded for peace and stability. Wars there
could not fail to be, but Sforza wanted them local, petty, and
circumscribed.

The dukes of Milan became an accepted fact in the major
state-system of Italy as Francesco Sforza completed the work
Gian Galeazzo Visconti had begun. No condottiere had won
such a prize as Francesco; and the tough captain who had once
stood amazed by the luxury of Pavia and the splendor of its
library now enjoyed the prosperity his sword had brought him.
War or no war, the Milanese throve. Francesco settled his court
at Milan, the heart of his dukedom, ruling his subjects until his
death in 1466 as he had once led his troops—wisely, directly,
decisively—always keeping within the limits of the possible.
About him there was something of the inexorable single-mind-
edness of the long-distance runner. Unhappily, his children
proved more devious, more extravagant, more brutal even than
their Visconti ancestors. The Sforza brood would have done
honor to the pages of the most blood-thirsty of Elizabethan
dramatists. And the story of Milan and its Renaissance reaches
a climax in the rule of Lodovico Sforza.

Francesco was a great warrior—in love as well as in war—
and his brood of Sforza, legitimate and illegitimate (the differ-

ence in Renaissance Italy was scarcely remarked—Francesco himself was a bastard), numbered twenty. Lodovico was number six (legitimate), so his prospects of the throne of Milan were remote enough. He possessed, however, one card, spurious perhaps, but not without value: he was the first legitimate child to be born *after* Francesco had been acclaimed Duke of Milan. Its use, however, lay in the future, for his brother Galeazzo Maria Sforza had every intention of enjoying to the full the power and the riches which his father had bequeathed him. Indeed, his court left no doubt that the Sforza had arrived, that the wealth of Milan was vast, that neither the Doge in Venice, the Pope in Rome, the Medici in Florence, nor the Aragonese kings in Naples could outvie them in magnificence. The great Castello Sforzesco, built like the Tower of London on the verge of the city—a convenience which fulfilled both the needs of strategy and sport—witnessed some of the most remarkable spectacles of the fifteenth century. Galeazzo loved shows. He made St. George's Day the great military spectacle of the year; tournaments, pageants, processions gave his mania full rein, and he thought nothing of ordering a thousand or more special liveries in costly velvet to put on his servants' backs. A greater pleasure still was to take a visiting prince or ambassador to his jewel house, Galeazzo's special pride and joy, where rubies, emeralds, sapphires, and diamonds lay in heaps—a treasure which King Christian of Denmark somewhat churlishly called "unbefitting a true and generous prince." Galeazzo, however, possessed a taste for more refined delights: his interest in music led him to comb Flanders, let alone Italy, for the singers who were almost the dominating passion of his life. Almost, but not quite: undoubtedly Galeazzo's greatest pleasures were drawn from the enjoyment of his courtiers' wives and the exercise of his personal power; and neither endeared him to his subjects. The latter, in fact, was his undoing. Rumors of his cruelty were inflated to the heights of a Gothic fairy tale, and rendered just

as macabre by the Duke's pious, almost morbid, insistence on
the strictest observance of religious ritual. So perhaps it was
not entirely unfitting that his assassins should have dispatched
him in church. They were a typical Renaissance bunch—a pen-
niless noble adventurer, a cousin who resented the rape of his
sister, an old, very disreputable master of rhetoric who had
preached too ardently, and practiced too publicly, the Greek
way of life, and a youthful republican intoxicated by the concept of tyrannicide, who, as he was slowly and carefully torn
to pieces, murmured, *"Mors acerba fama perpetua est."*

Galeazzo's wife was deeply troubled that her husband, whom
she knew so well, should have been dispatched unconfessed.
She made a list of his sins and was appalled. He was, she
wrote, "Versed in warfare, both lawful and unlawful; in pillage, robbery, and devastation of the country; in extortion of
subjects; in negligence of justice; in injustice knowingly committed; in the imposition of new taxes which even included the
clergy; in carnal vices; in notorious and scandalous simony and
innumerable other crimes." Obviously the torments of Galeazzo
in Purgatory would be long and grievous, so the Duchess im-
plored the aid of the Pope. The Pope, moved by the distress of
the widow, granted absolution in return for a considerable
subsidy for the papal army.

Galeazzo left a child and five brothers; so the years after
his death proved dramatic enough for Milan and Italy. Conspiracies in Genoa and Parma linked themselves with greater
conspiracies, engineered by the Pope and the King of Naples,
in Florence. Lodovico tried his utmost to kidnap the child
Duke, but he failed until the ructions in Florence gave him
the backing of the Holy Father and King Ferrante. With luck
and good judgment, aided by the silliness of the Duke's mother
and the misguided cunning of her lover, Lodovico became
regent of Milan. He imprisoned the Duchess, ousted her favorite, and chopped off the head of Cecco Simonetta, the brilliant

ducal secretary who throughout his long life had devotedly served the Sforza, for the crime of attempting to secure an undivided inheritance for the legitimate heir. Fortunately for Lodovico, his most active and ambitious brothers had died during the struggle for power, and his nephew proved so weak in intellect and character that it was unnecessary to dispatch him. As soon as this internecine struggle was over, Milan settled down to such spectacular festivities that they pushed the memories of Galeazzo's junketings to the commonplace. The child Duke was betrothed to Isabella of Aragon, and Lodovico himself took Beatrice d'Este, the daughter of the Duke of Ferrara and granddaughter of the King of Naples, for his bride. Although their marriages were long delayed, the festivities celebrating their nuptials provided the hired chroniclers of the court of Milan, long practiced in rhetoric and panegyric, a subject worthy of their hyperbole. Men and women were dressed, or rather undressed, as pagan gods and goddesses; fabulous animals were wondrously contrived; knights jousted in Moorish costumes; wild men, dressed by Leonardo da Vinci, scared the ladies; dwarfs, giants, hunchbacks provided robust fun; sycophantic poets produced verse by the ream to give a sense of immortal occasion; the best musicians of Milan, and they were certainly the best in Italy, played and sang through the day and night; masques with elaborate scenery and ingenious fireworks linked the intervals between Gargantuan banquets. The prodigious munificence of Lodovico naturally stirred the interest of painters, sculptors, engineers, historians, philosophers, and poets. Leonardo, frustrated and restless in Florence, was one of the first to seek his patronage.

Lodovico's extravagance was not mere self-indulgence. He wished to demonstrate not only the wealth and power of the Milanese state but also his own supreme control. He was a highly intelligent man with a deep sense of cunning, who realized acutely the insecurity of his realm as well as of his dynasty.

Prosperity, he thought, would cure the former, diplomacy the latter. He cultivated the rich Lombard plain assiduously. He promoted canals. He encouraged new crops, particularly rice. He fostered trade and manufacture. And his interest in Leonardo da Vinci owed as much to the artist's inventive genius in mechanics and fortifications as to his ability as a sculptor and painter. By such means he created the sinews of power, but its exploitation depended on his wit.

Milan's dangers were these: firstly Venice, secondly France, thirdly the Holy Roman Emperor, and fourthly the Swiss, who could be manipulated by the others. Milan had been intermittently at war with Venice since the Venetians decided to become a mainland power at the beginning of the fifteenth century. The problems represented by the Emperor and France were interrelated. For Lodovico's Visconti ancestors, the Emperor had been a safety factor, since they were his legal representatives in Lombardy. The Sforza were not, however, and the legal basis of their power had to rest on popular acclamation. To complicate the matter further, the Visconti had intermarried with the junior branches of the French royal family, and this had given the French certain dynastic claims on Milan. Furthermore, the French had always coveted Genoa, which was a linchpin of the Milanese economy; and they supported the Anjou pretensions to the throne of Naples. To create some stability in this world fraught with danger, Lodovico, Lorenzo de' Medici, and Ferrante, the King of Naples, had enacted the Triple Alliance. Together they had been able to present the threat of sufficient force to make external or internal powers hesitate to attack them. War had not been abolished, but certainly the Triple Alliance diminished it, and Lodovico was the beneficiary. Milan had other reasons than the Triple Alliance for friendship with Naples. Ties between the two cities had been strengthened by the marriage of the young Duke and Ferrante's granddaughter, Isabella of Aragon. Or so it would seem. Reasons of state and reasons of strategy were at variance, however, with Lodovico's personal ambition. He wished to be Duke of Milan, *de jure* as well as *de facto*. That meant setting aside, or killing, the young Duke, whose wife already bitterly resented the anomaly of her position and the slights, real and imagined, from Lodovico's wife—the intelligent, formidable, and far from discreet Beatrice d'Este. Behind the wronged wife, Naples could be arrayed; so might France, for the Duke of Orléans had better dynastic claims than Lodovico; so might the Emperor, who could bestow his Vicariate on whomsoever he wished. In so complex a situation Lodovico worked his astrologers hard, and the conjunction and combination of the stars became his daily concern. The point of desperation was reached when his nephew came of age and fathered an heir before Beatrice d'Este produced a son for Lodovico. The arrival of an heir to the dukedom was received with modest celebrations, and much to Isabella's fury the banquets, jousts, pageants, and *Te Deums* that celebrated the birth of Lodovico's son were as splendiferous as they were prolonged. No doubt remained as to how the Regent's mind was working.

Lodovico's opportunity came when Charles VIII of France, who had acquired the Anjou claims to the Neapolitan throne, having settled his quarrel with the Emperor, thought that he might exercise his nobility and seek honor and reward by invading Naples. This seeming act of folly Lodovico encouraged; and in return for his benevolent neutrality Charles supported Lodovico's claim to the Emperor to be appointed Imperial Vicar of Milan—a legitimization of power never yet won by a Sforza. A further piece of luck—as no doubt the stars had foretold—took place. His nephew, the Duke, died. Lodovico proclaimed the infant Francesco duke. Not surprisingly, the Council would not have him; they begged Lodovico, at such a time of peril for the state, to assume the title with the power. Lodovico complied; the populace cheered. So Lodovico achieved his *coup d'état*—a bloodless one and timed to perfection. In his campaign against Naples, Charles VIII proved almost miraculously successful (as is common with military miracles, it was based on superior armament, particularly cannon). With Charles thus occupied and the imperial edict safe in his pocket, Lodovico suddenly changed sides, and when Charles began to withdraw from Italy, Sforza was one of those who harried and hurried him on his way. Then, sensing the possible benefits, he seized the opportune moment to switch allegiance to Charles once again.

So Lodovico had his years of triumph. He could boast that the Pope was his chaplain, the Emperor his condottiere, Venice his chamberlain, and the King of France his courier. For a time Milan was prosperous, the court brilliant, the prince magnificent. And then death took a hand. Beatrice, who had done so much to bring Lodovico's subtleties to decisive action, died in childbed. Charles VIII of France also died; his successor, Louis XII, claimed Milan and regarded Charles VIII's failure to take it for him as a disgrace. Apart from Naples, which feared a fresh invasion, the powers of Italy leaped as rapidly as possible onto the French bandwagon (Venice alone bargaining hard for its ticket) and were overjoyed that the victim beneath the juggernaut's wheels should be Lodovico. The French won; Lodovico retreated to the Tirol; the French puppet outraged the Milanese; Lodovico returned; so did the French, and won again with consummate ease. This time they packed Lodovico off to France, where his imprisonment was strict enough to titillate the most morbid humanist, obsessed with the fate of tyrants. He finally died in a tiny, lightless, underground cell in the dungeon of Loches.

It was not the end of the Sforza. They had become pawns in the battle between the great European powers who used Lombardy as their tilting ground. Sforza's son, Massimiliano, was brought back by the lances of the Swiss, and after a brief and extrava-

gant career he was removed, after the Battle of Marignano, by
Francis I and pensioned, not imprisoned, in France. These two
wars, which devastated Milan, were soon followed by a third,
when Charles V, who combined the formidable power of his
Holy Roman Empire with that of Spain, decided to expel the
French from Lombardy. This he did in 1525 outside the great
Visconti capital of Pavia. It was a fitting place, for with that
battle the last gleams of Milanese independence disappeared.
The reason for this tale of blood is not far to seek. Although
Milan possessed natural frontiers and great wealth and an able
ruling house, as a state it never acquired the stability of Florence or Venice or even Naples, simply because its class struggles went unresolved. The feudal nobility were never uprooted;
they constantly quarreled with each other and provided a ready
support for any adventurer, internal or external, who would
favor their personal ambitions. This powerful aristocracy also
thrived on the divisions and jealousies of the merchant class
which hated it. Finally, Milan was hemmed about with cities
almost as great as itself, all possessing rich, ambitious, jealous
guilds of merchants who seesawed between wanting the stability
which the leadership of Milan alone could bring and the gain
that might accrue from its humiliation. In such an unstable
world the abilities of the Visconti and the Sforza were largely
wasted. The great horse designed by Leonardo for Lodovico
in memory of his father seems curiously symbolic of their
destiny—conceived in grandeur, executed in clay, never cast,
ruined by the French, and destroyed by time.

VI

ROME

SPLENDOR AND THE PAPACY

Rome was a city caught, like an old man, in memories, delusions, and dreams. Even when fighting (and not too successfully at that) the little town of Tivoli, medals were struck bearing the proud title, *Roma caput mundi:* Rome, the world's ruler. By 1400, however, even the great days of the Middle Ages seemed remote to realistic men, and gone forever. For most of the fourteenth century the popes had lived at Avignon in France, in the great and luxurious Palais des Papes that looms above the Rhone, where the broken Roman bridge became a symbol of the Church's break with its own past. To Avignon went the clerics, lawyers, and merchants who harvested and spent the wealth which a pious Europe poured into the papal lap. It was to Avignon that Francesco Datini, the famous merchant of Prato, went to make his fortune as a small but ambitious boy of fifteen. And make it he did, in his determined, hardheaded, Tuscan way, selling silks, jewels, works of art, damasks, swords, silverware, cloth, even salt—anything that would make the money grow, although the profits on his insurance and his banking interests nagged at his conscience. Through men like Datini, Avignon prospered and Rome lost; and, of course, the artists too went where the money was, and Sienese artists painted the frescoes that adorned the Palace's walls.

True, in Rome a few cardinals still flaunted their courtesans, and a few saintly men continued to dedicate themselves to the liturgical worship of God and the relief of the poor. Even the Curia functioned, although ever more slowly. But the absence of the Papacy was killing Rome as inexorably as a cancer. The vast ruinous buildings, combined with constant plague, stifled hope, depressed the spirit, bred despair. In this dark world the great, furious Roman tribes—the Orsini, the Colonna, the Frangipani—made their sport, and what a sport it was! They tossed each other into the Tiber, and when a pope ventured to enter Rome, they chased him into the fortress of Sant'Angelo or frightened him—like the aged Gregory XII—into the remoter corners of the Patrimony. They terrorized the citizens, raped the nuns, robbed the monks, pillaged the churches. To compound confusion, from 1378 to 1429 there was an antipope as well as a pope, and in 1409 even three authentic successors of St. Peter—a glorious opportunity for rebellion, riot, and plunder. King Ladislas of Naples prowled about the broken-down streets of Rome, extorting what he could and decapitating whom he dared. Popes and kings hired the toughest, most brutal condottieri—including Braccio, who, according to a chronicler, enjoyed the sufferings of others, and for his pleasure would throw a few men from the highest towers in Rome or drop a prisoner into a boiling cauldron. After years of anarchy the Romans were willing to believe anything and nothing. When John XXIII, afterwards struck from the list of the popes and accused of a huge catalogue of crimes, the least important of which were incest, sodomy, and murder, swore that he would defend them to the death, they replied that they would rather eat their children than surrender to his enemies. During the same night John XXIII flew under the cover of darkness, taking all the portable wealth he could lay his hands on, and the Romans opened their gates the next morning, their children undevoured. Such a kaleidoscope of brutality, such a cascade of violence, broke the government of the city in pieces and reduced it to a poverty and a misery it had not known since the barbarian invasions.

No one in 1425 could have foreseen that Rome was about to be reborn (not spiritually—the Renaissance popes were not to prove men of the spirit—but physically, artistically, and politically). St. Peter's, the Vatican, the churches, the tombs, the squares, the great palaces and gardens of Rome which now entrance the eye and delight the heart, were brought into being and gave an impetus to the pursuit of beauty that the stern moralities of the Counter Reformation could not stop. For two hundred years the beauty of Rome became the pride of the Papacy. The downward plunge into anarchy and destitution and poverty was checked by Martin V, himself a Colonna and a Roman. During his pontificate (1417–1431) the dreadful split in the Church was cured, if not quite healed. Furthermore, he proved a good administrator and such a fearsome personality that he secured peace for the city. He checked the robberies, violence, and murder, and stimulated the city's trade. With the papal court back in Rome, back came the pilgrims and supplicants, back came the merchants, and back came the lifeblood— the papal tax harvest that was reaped from Europe's peasantry. And so the Roman soil was fertilized again, for without wealth no Renaissance was possible. The next pope, Eugenius IV, had to flee down the Tiber in a rowboat, disguised as a monk, and eluded capture only by a hair's breadth. For years he kept his court at Florence, where he patronized the humanists and bided his time, while he left Rome to be pacified by a ferocious bishop, Vitelleschi, who razed cities, hanged and decapitated barons, slaughtered right, left, and center, and probably met his own end by poison (possibly with Eugenius' connivance). By such murderous methods were the popes re-established. The calculated savageries of Cesare Borgia, that were to astound a later generation, were unusual only in the beauty and dexterity of their timing.

To be secure in Rome, the Papacy needed to control the States of the Church which stretched in a broad diagonal across the long leg of Italy. During its residence at Avignon and the Great Schism (1378 to 1417), men and cities had naturally usurped papal rights and privileges, and what they had won by force they would not yield by persuasion. Excommunication, interdict, or anathema left them unmoved. These had been flung about so wantonly by rival popes at each other that they had lost much of their force. Indeed, it seemed to the popes that the Church could only get back its own by acting like any other power in Italy. By alliance, by diplomacy, by war, the Church might wrest its possessions from alien hands. Its wealth permitted it to hire the ablest condottieri, including the great Francesco Sforza as well as Federigo da Montefeltro. Having been a plaything of the great powers, the leaders of the Church wished to secure independence by giving the Church great temporal and political strength. That being so, they looked for a leader not among the saints nor usually among the scholars (Nicholas V and Pius II were exceptions) but among the administrators and natural politicians. They looked for worldly men, men of powerful personalities, tough fiber, and quick decision. And again, as the power of the Papacy steadily grew through temporal measures such as war and diplomacy, so did the need for such qualities in a pope seem ever more necessary. This is the explanation of what so many now find difficult to understand—of popes such as Alexander VI or Julius II. Alexander VI, whose lusts repelled even the tolerant age in which he lived, was a very hardheaded diplomat and excellent administrator, whose policy undeviatingly pursued what was thought to be a necessity for the Church—temporal power, expressed in the overlordship of central Italy. Julius II, even as pope, loved war, loved to get on his horse, to feel the weight of his armor and hear the blood-call of battle.

So, by and large, the Renaissance popes were worldly men, pragmatic, tough, concerned with power. And like many hardheaded, ambitious men they did not wish to be outshone by their rivals in the symbolic display of wealth and greatness. They were determined to build vast churches, huge palaces, magnificent fountains; to employ the finest painters, sculptors, craftsmen; to collect the loveliest antiquities, the most resplendent jewels, the most remarkable books, the most exquisite manuscripts. These things, like their armies, were necessities of state, and the cost irrelevant. So hand in hand with the resurgent power of the Papacy went the artistic Renaissance in Rome; and because the popes controlled more wealth, the result was more splendid than anywhere else.

Rome was full of priests, monks, nuns, churches, monasteries, convents, holy relics, miraculous shrines, healing images. Every year thousands of pilgrims from all corners of the Western world made their way to it in penitence and in hope. Most were simple people to whom the sight of a piece of the True Cross or a saint's leg justified the dangers and tribulations of their journey. They cared nothing for the whispered rumors of the Pope's children, of his poisonings, murders, or even the alarming sensualities of the Borgia. Twenty thousand of them reverenced Alexander VI in the great Jubilee year of 1500—unmindful of his lusts. For them the mounting grandeur of Rome was a wondrous thing, a visible proof of the glory of their Church. Humanist criticism of the Church's venality, corruption, immorality, and obscurantism fell on deaf ears. A Savonarola or a Bernardino of Siena might momentarily stir this multitude with a sense of the world's unrighteousness, but the vast mass of the Western world was locked in an accepting piety, and the luminous sins of the popes and cardinals were a matter for gossip but not for radical rage. Throughout the Renaissance, with its political and personal immorality and its intellectual skepticism, Rome remained the center of the Western world's religion. From this atmosphere of worship no pope could escape, and it became subtly interwoven in the Renaissance in Rome.

There is no need to follow the twists and turns by which the Papacy gradually re-established its dominion over the Patrimony or to describe how from time to time this was endangered by popes trying to create hereditary dominions for their children (Cesare Borgia, for example), a tendency which scores of Orsini and Colonna died bloody deaths to prevent. The treaties, battles, and plots have faded to near-oblivion; there remain, however, in all their greatness, the treasures of the Vatican, its library, its antiquities, its sculptures, its paintings. And the Vatican is but a fragment of Renaissance Rome; the *Laocoön* and the *Apollo Belvedere* belong to it as much as St. Peter's or Via Giulia, for a reverence for her own past grew with her new delight in beauty.

The revival of Rome began, like the Renaissance itself, with literature. The Italian Papacy, at the time of the Schism, had many Tuscans in its service, among them Poggio, one of the luckiest of the humanists. After Petrarch's discovery of lost letters of Cicero the search for ancient manuscripts intensified, and Poggio's instinct seemed to lead him unerringly to his target like a pig to truffles. Perhaps he was more thorough, more remorseless than the rest; whatever the cause, his haul was prodigious. In the Swiss monastery of St. Gall he unearthed the entire works of Quintilian; other highlights of his discoveries were the poems of Lucretius, discourses by Cicero, treatises on architecture by Vitruvius and on agriculture by Columella. The rich patrons of Italy rushed to buy them or to have them exquisitely copied and illuminated, for the competition to possess first-rate classical manuscripts splendidly illuminated was as keen as that for French impressionists among present-day millionaires. Tommaso Parentucelli, the son of a surgeon, who became Nicholas V, was as addicted to books as the Borgia family was to women. "What was unknown to Parentucelli," said Pius II, "lay outside the sphere of human learning." He encouraged his secretaries to ransack old monastic libraries, and he employed an army of copyists. Terrified by the fall of Constantinople, he sent his emissaries scurrying to Greece and collected a few Greek codices at vast expense. He paid extravagant prices for the work of translation as well as for the books themselves: indeed, he offered ten thousand gold pieces for a fine translation of Homer. He employed the best of all classical scholars, Lorenzo Valla, who had proved some of the most hallowed documents in the papal Curia to be forgeries. As well as being a destructive scholar of genius, Valla was a satirist with the bite of acid, and his favorite targets were priests, monks, and cardinals. In fact, during the pontificate of Eugenius IV, Rome had been too hot for him. Nicholas V welcomed him and employed him. And, of course, the Pope created a fitting setting for his great library: the books were housed in the Vatican and exquisitely bound in red velvet with silver clasps. Philosophers, rhetoricians, poets, historians, philologists, grammarians, and teachers of Latin and Greek all were welcome in the new palace of the Vatican that Nicholas was creating, whether their work fortified or undermined the authority of the Papacy. Only a few setbacks marred the triumphant development which Nicholas had started. As with so many aspects of the Renaissance, Sixtus IV was also involved in the extension and adornment of the Vatican library. Even Alexander VI added to it, although his interest in learning, and it was a genuine one, expressed itself in the patronage of the University of Rome. Between them Nicholas and Sixtus laid the foundations, and secured some of the rarest treasures, of the greatest library in the Western world.

Although the reverence of most popes for the literature of antiquity was profound, their attitude toward the visible remains of ancient Rome was more haphazard. The collection of coins, of bronzes, and of statuary had been the cult of a few cardinals even as early as 1400; and naturally, as the fashion for antiquity spread, so did the desire to acquire genuine works of art of classical Rome and Greece. But the vast ruins of Rome were a different matter. The huge Palatine Hill, upon which had stood the immense palaces of the emperors, had become an incoherent mass of rubble—broken arches, paths, and masonry covered in sage and thyme and rosemary, crowned with olive trees, and grazed by sheep. It was a desolate, rural place—a paradise only for the meditative humanist brooding on the mortality of greatness. The Arch of Constantine was buried in ruins and covered by houses; the Colosseum was a mound of tumbled marble; everywhere there were broken columns, remains of theaters, circuses, stadiums; and medieval houses spread like weeds in and out and over this ruined city. These crapulous vestiges of a glorious past were harder to cherish, and although an occasional pope paid lip service to the need for their preservation and issued Bulls for it, the majority happily plundered them for building materials or razed them to the ground for their new projects. Nicholas V removed 2,300 wagon loads of marble from the Colosseum in a single year, as well as quarrying from the Circus Maximus, the Forum, the Arch of Titus, and the Temple of Venus. Even that great patron and connoisseur Sixtus IV took stones from ancient buildings and built a bridge across the Tiber from the masonry of the Colosseum. A few dedicated men, like the great architect Brunelleschi, dug and measured and drew the ancient buildings; but most men were drawn to them, like the robbers of the pyramids, by the hope of a lucky find, for the search for antiquities had revealed masterpiece after masterpiece of ancient art, culminating in 1490 in the discovery of the *Apollo Belvedere* in a Roman villa. Even if the great plundered the ruins or ignored them, there were humble scholars whom they fascinated, and the best of these was Ciriaco de' Pizzicolli who wandered throughout the classical world, measuring, sketching, describing the visible remains of antiquity. Antiquarian studies, however, were largely confined to medals, coins, inscriptions, marbles, and bronzes, things which could be collected and displayed: there were, of course, not enough, and forgeries soon abounded, to the confusion and despair of posterity.

Although the popes had little wish to preserve, as in aspic, the ruins of Rome, they dearly desired to restore its architectural supremacy. The popes recovered a ruined city shrunk to a tiny area of Imperial Rome, and fields and orchards and wild, overgrown places abounded. Nicholas V, fortunately, possessed a touch of megalomania; fortunately, because size and space are vital principles of architectural splendor. He not only dreamed, but also planned, a vast new Rome, dominated by a new St. Peter's, a new papal palace, and protected by an invincible Castel Sant'Angelo. The medieval popes had lived in the indefensible and oft-burned Palace of St. John Lateran, but on their return from Avignon it was so ruinous that they had taken up residence in the Vatican Palace, which had been the guest palace for emperors and kings. Nicholas V sent for the great Florentine architects Rossellino and Alberti, men totally hostile to the Gothic, and as addicted as the Pope to classical antiquity. All the gold and silver of the West would scarcely have been sufficient for the multitude of churches, convents, monasteries, palaces, theaters, gardens, piazzas, towers, walls, and fortifications which they planned. The cost did not daunt the Pope. He tore down the ancient Roman temples near St. Peter's and began slowly to lay the foundations of his new basilica. At his death the whole of what is now the Vatican City was scarred with trenches for the huge walls of his dreams. They were never fulfilled, but Sixtus IV, Alexander VI, Julius II, and Leo X completed the destruction of medieval Rome and created the new city of the Renaissance that was to prove worthy of him.

Sixtus IV, born in poverty, ruthlessly pursued greatness. Sensual, self-indulgent, decisive, an excellent administrator and generous patron, he is in many ways the most typical of Renaissance popes. He showered gold on his nephews (one of whom was to become pope as Julius II) and stopped short of no means to get his political ends. He helped to promote the Pazzi conspiracy and, in fury at its failure, placed Florence under the Interdict. His personal immorality gave rise to the wildest rumors; but the lack of restraint in the satisfaction of his appetites provoked an extravagance that was entirely beneficent for posterity. Not since the days of the emperors had Rome witnessed such junketings. Here is a description of the food at the banquet given by Sixtus when a bastard daughter of the King of Naples arrived in Rome to meet her future husband: "Before them were carried wild boars, roasted whole in their entire hides, bucks, goats, hares, rabbits, fish silvered over, peacocks with their feathers, pheasants, storks, cranes and stags; a bear in its skin, holding in its mouth a stick; countless were the tarts, jellies, candied fruits and sweetmeats. An artificial mountain was carried into the room, out of which stepped a liveryman with gestures of surprise at finding himself in the midst of such a gorgeous banquet; he repeated some verses and then vanished. Mythological figures served as covers to the viands placed on the table. The history of Atlas, of Perseus and Andromeda, the labors of Hercules were depicted life size on silver dishes. Castles made of sweetmeats and filled with eatables were sacked and then thrown from the loggia of the hall to the applauding crowd. Sailing vessels discharged their cargoes of sugared almonds . . ." By such means, perhaps, Sixtus obliterated the memories of his hungry youth, but many of his indulgences were less transitory. His taste in building was as simple and as austere as his delight in food was riotous and fantastic. He widened streets, constructed bridges, built hospitals, erected churches, gave land to all who would build houses and palaces. He encouraged his cardinals to foster the splendor of Rome: the market was expelled from the Piazza Navona and the building of its churches and palaces begun. There was scarcely a ward of the city that Sixtus did not improve or adorn, but his greatest glory is the chapel in the Vatican that bears his name. Utterly simple in design, it served merely as a frame for its adornment, and for this purpose Sixtus brought the best artists in Italy to Rome—Signorelli, Botticelli, Perugino, Pinturicchio, Ghirlandaio, Rosselli. Later, in the pontificate of Julius II, who wished to complete his uncle's work, these frescoes were dwarfed by the superb ceiling by Michelangelo, for which the Sistine Chapel is so famous. Such, however, was the galaxy of painters in Rome in the 1470's that they founded their own guild, that of St. Luke, which afterwards developed into the famous academy. Although painters and sculptors and architects had been patronized by the popes long before Nicholas V and Sixtus IV (Giotto had created mosaics and painted frescoes for the old St. Peter's, and Fra Angelico had adorned many churches), yet with their pontificates papal patronage moved into a new dimension. It touched all aspects of art and learning. Possessing great wealth and sublime authority, many of the popes rose to the enormous visions of Nicholas V. The Basilica of St. Peter's—the work not of one but of a plethora of geniuses: Alberti, Bramante, Raphael, Michelangelo, Bernini —is the most impressive Christian monument in the world, yet it is essentially a product of the Renaissance. The treasures of the Vatican Palace—paintings, sculpture, antiquities, ancient manuscripts, and rare books—are incomparable, yet in 1420 the Papacy possessed no more perhaps than three hundred books, and scarcely any antiquities or pictures or statues of merit. To sensual, warlike, popes who ruled from 1471 to 1521 Rome owes a great deal of its present beauty.

What a strange gallery these popes make, yet essentially they are as much creatures of the Renaissance as Michelangelo's *Adam* or Donatello's *David*. The strangest of all is doubtless Alexander VI, whose name has become a byword for lust and cruelty. Certainly he was a man of strong, animal passions, driven remorselessly by his instincts. His attachment to his mistress, Vannozza, who bore him the terrible Borgia brood, was profound and life-lasting, no matter what other temporary indulgence he permitted himself. He loved his children to desperation, with a fierce physical passion. When one son was stabbed and thrown into the Tiber, probably by another son, Cesare

Borgia, his grief astounded the cardinals whom he called to a consistory in order to bewail the loss of his child. So deep was his grief that, in tears, he swore not only to reform his own life, but also the Church's. His animal spirits, however, soon reasserted themselves, and his slavish devotion to his son Cesare became the bane of Italy when he resolved to create for him a great Italian kingdom. After spectacular victories in which, with French aid, Cesare overcame the great seemingly impregnable fortresses of the Romagna, as well as Urbino, he seemed to Machiavelli to be the destined ruler of Italy. Machiavelli admired the way Cesare welcomed his enemies as friends and then neatly strangled them. By such stratagems were the Orsini obliterated. The speed, the decision, the timing of Cesare had an almost physical perfection. Yet, as in some Greek tragedy, the fates kept a bitter end in store. Before Cesare could consolidate his power, his father died; at the time he himself was prostrated with a loathsome and debilitating sickness. Stripped of power, he became a pawn of popes, kept on sufferance, banished to prison in Spain, and finally was killed in a brawl in Navarre. The life of Alexander's daughter, Lucrezia, was marked by a similar irony of fate. The Pope loved her with an almost incestuous passion. He heaped wealth on her; no delight was too sumptuous or too lascivious to be denied her. No husband was worthy of her charms: one was declared impotent by Papal Bull; one was assassinated. But Lucrezia lived on long after her father's death, her life threated with tragedy and stultified by a wearisome piety that mocked her past. The depth and ferocity of the Pope's passion for his children have made him an ogre of history, making men forget his astonishing dignity, his overwhelming physical charm, and the immense presence as well as that animal vitality which made him as unwearying at work as at pleasure, and the bull his proper emblem. His irresponsible virility was scarcely in keeping with the tiara, but his pontificate was far from disastrous for the

Papacy. He brought its temporal possessions more firmly under its control, and even though his intention to transfer these temporalities to his own family would, if realized, have ruined the Church, yet the possibility that this could be achieved was so remote that the success of Cesare merely redounded to the advantage of the Papacy.

That advantage was brilliantly exploited by Julius II. Sixty years old when he was elected pope, he possessed the strength and decision of a man half his years. He loved action, hated the French, loathed the great Roman families, not one member of which he elevated to the purple, and detested the tyrants of Perugia and Bologna who usurped the temporal power of his Church. Defeat merely increased his energy, and in all his dealings this tough, thickset priest was bold, decisive, and single-minded. His aim was the absolute independence of the Papacy from emperors, kings, or Romans, for without that temporal independence its claims to universality in a world of national states, he realized, would be meaningless. As in politics, so in art, Julius never vacillated. Nor did he play safe. Hearing of the abilities of the young Raphael, he sent for him from Florence, ordered him to obliterate paintings by Piero della Francesca, Signorelli, Perugino, Sodoma, and the rest and to cover the walls of the rooms now known as the Stanze of Raphael with subjects of his own choice. The result is one of the great glories of Renaissance Rome. In architecture Julius showed the same sweeping vision, the same decisive action. He patronized Bramante, a man whose dreams were as grandiose as Julius could wish, accepted his colossal plans with alacrity, and taxed the faithful. Nor was it in any way surprising that Julius, who always stared life directly in the eye, should contemplate death with the same robust realism. Michelangelo's designs for his tomb entranced him; after all, it was the largest and most ornate mausoleum conceived in Europe since Theodoric's, but he could not bridle his impatience with the sculp-

tor's slow progress, his creative doubts and endless reconsidera-
tions, which drove the Pope to such furious quarrels that
Michelangelo left Rome in anger and the project came to a
standstill. Nor did reconciliation speed it forward—long after
his death, a part of Julius' tomb went up in the little church of
San Pietro in Vincoli; his bones lie in an undistinguished grave
in the Vatican. Julius' furious spirit did not always meet such
adamantine opposition.

The triumph of the Renaissance Papacy received its most
splendid illustration in the coronation of Julius' successor—the
young Giovanni de' Medici, son of Lorenzo, who became pope
in 1513, at the age of thirty-seven. Bull-necked, popeyed, red-
faced, he totally lacked the presence and ferocity of an Alexander VI or a Julius II. The cardinals in conclave had decided
to avoid aggressive, virile temperaments. They had had enough
of them. Leo X belied his name. Subtle, intuitive, sophisticated,
he charmed with his generosity, affability, and sweetness of
manner. Discretion veiled his private life, and his character and
his education gave him a range of intellectual interests and
sympathies not matched by a pope since Nicholas V. Bred in
riches and nurtured in luxury, he had no compunction in using
the wealth of the Church in splendiferous pageantry. Since the
days of the emperors the Romans had never witnessed a procession comparable to his, as it made its way from the Vatican to
St. John Lateran. Cardinals and bankers vied with each other
in the display of artistic treasures or the construction of ceremonial arches. Agostino Chigi erected an eight-column arch
and festooned it with his best pictures and sculpture. Apollos,
Ganymedes, Bacchuses, Minervas, Venuses, nymphs and dryads,
emperors and princes, the best antiquities that Rome had to
offer lined the Via Triumphalis, sharing it with the newly
painted apostles and prophets of Christendom. The procession
itself equaled its setting. Two hundred and fifty abbots, bishops,
patriarchs, and cardinals were matched by the representatives

of Italy's great families. The Gonzaga, Este, Sforza, Bentivoglio, Colonna, Orsini, Baglioni, nobles of Florence, patricians from Venice, knights from the Romagna, the Duke of Urbino in black velvet, Lucrezia Borgia's husband released from excommunication for the occasion, and the rebel Cardinal, Alfonso Petrucci, whom Leo, four years later, was to have executed, were set like jewels amidst chamberlains, standard-bearers, guards, and acolytes. On that day passions were buried, no stones were hurled, no angry shouts drowned the plainsong, no daggers flashed in the cruel sun. All paid homage to the fat, perspiring, red-faced Pope, clad in white, sitting sidesaddle on his white palfrey. Eighty years earlier no pope could have risked his life and throne in such a spectacle.

Although Rome steadily increased in splendor, and the Pope's authority waxed majestic, violence, turmoil, and chicanery still threaded the papal annals with the scarlet of battle and murder. Enemies of papal power abounded: the French, the Spaniards, and the Milanese had found no resolution to their dynastic ambitions, and the Venetians had not given up their belief that security could only be achieved by raping the Church of its northeastern temporalities. What was more, the wealth of the Church proved insufficient for its needs. Taxes grew grievous, the sale of indulgences more blatant. Across the Alps criticism of clerical worldliness, of monkish foolishness, of papal avarice, of Roman decadence, had often been sharp and prolonged. Under the stimulus of national needs, criticism developed a political and social purpose. And Luther, who might easily have met his end at the stake like another Savonarola, became the founder of a reformed Christianity that came to see the Pope as Antichrist and Rome as the whore of Babylon. The tribulations of the Reformation dimmed the luster of the Papacy; yet the heretic Germans were remote and their future uncertain, and it was a more immediate tragedy that jolted the Romans and the Church out of the gilded sweetness of Medicean rule into a sterner, harsher world. In 1527 the soldiers of the great Hapsburg ruler Charles V, whose dominions embraced the Spanish as well as the German Empire, sacked Rome efficiently, brutally, completely. After the death of Clement VII, another Medici who succeeded Leo X, the growing rift with Protestantism and the shock left by the devastation of Rome bred a sterner spirit in the Church and Papacy. The more flamboyant aspects of the Renaissance were suppressed: speculation went out of fashion; dogma was more sharply defined at the great Council of Trent; the Holy Office and the Index maintained its purity; the new order of Jesuits soon dominated the school and the confessional, and men of ruthless will and unbending morality sat on the throne of Saint Peter, marshaling and leading the resurgent forces of Catholicism. They deplored paganism; repressed the licentiousness of the Romans, religious and secular; insisted on sacred subjects in art and clapped fig leaves on the statues of antiquity. So great, however, was the impetus of the Renaissance that they could not stop it. For centuries Rome continued to grow in beauty, and became, as no other city, the embodiment of the arts, if not the spirit, of the Renaissance.

VII

VENICE

THE GOLDEN YEARS

On Ascension Day, 997, Doge Pietro Orseolo stayed his galleon
in the great sea-gateway that joins the Venetian lagoon with the
Adriatic, poured a libation on the sea, and received the blessing
of his Patriarch before he sallied forth to annihilate the Dal-
matians. For eight hundred years that ceremony was repeated,
growing in complexity and splendor as Venice herself grew
rich and powerful, until it became one of the great ritual pageants of the Western world. The huge state barge of the doges,
the *Bucentaur,* ablaze with crimson and cloth of gold, drew
away from the Piazzetta to the chants of massed choirs. The
Council of Ten, the Signory, the patricians and ambassadors,
followed in their gilded gondolas. At the Porto di Lido the
Doge, standing on the poop of the *Bucentaur,* cast a golden
ring into the waters, declaring "O sea, we wed thee in sign of
our true and everlasting dominion." The mixture of paganism,
Christianity, and Oriental splendor was as symbolic of Venice
as the marriage to the sea.

The sea linked Venice with Byzantium, the market for her
goods, the protector of her liberties, the model of her state, the
teacher of her crafts, the fountain of her arts. Under Byzantium's protecting wing Venice had grown to greatness,
great enough to rend and despoil the Empire in the Fourth
Crusade, yet not great enough to save the imperial city in its
days of crisis when, in 1453, the surge of the Turkish hordes

95

overwhelmed it. The loss proved grievous, but not disastrous, for by that time the sources of Venetian power were scattered throughout the seas of the Western world.

Venice lived by her ships. Thanks to them, the desolate mud flats had flowered in stone. To this strange water-borne city they brought riches, power, and security. Only twice in its history did enemy vessels sail into the waters of the Venetian lagoon, and both times the enemy was annihilated. To the landward its defenses proved equally inviolate. The Venetians made their ships in the great Arsenal that was the wonder of Europe in the Middle Ages. Its two miles of forbidding fortifications enclosed the most formidable armory in the Renaissance world. Thousands of workmen toiled there, and a new galley was produced every hundred days. These ships could be commissioned with amazing alacrity. From the Arsenal to the lagoon the ships moved as on a conveyerbelt—masts, sails, oars, stores, and weapons were quickly loaded as the vessel slowly passed each storehouse. Most fittings on each galley were standardized, so that replacements could be stored in all Venetian warehouses, whether they might be in Southampton or Tyre; any crew could be moved to any ship without further training, or a fresh crew could be made up from survivors in battle. And every galley, whether used in commerce or in war, belonged to the state: no patrician, no matter what his wealth might be, could possess a Venetian galley. Such precise regimentation, such absolute control, gave Venice its pre-eminence over its rivals and enabled it to ship a crusading army to the Holy Land without overstretching its resources. The other maritime powers of Italy hated the supremacy of Venice. Genoa ruined herself in a long and desperate war, which ranged from the Bosporus to the lagoon itself, in an attempt to crush Venice and despoil her of the riches which her great fleet carried for her merchants. By 1400 Venice had proved herself invicible; indeed, she had become the center of a sea-borne empire. Zara,

Ragusa, Crete, and many Aegean Islands belonged to her ab-
solutely: trading communities, enjoying extraterritorial privileges, had been established in Constantinople, Acre, Tyre,
Sidon, Alexandria. Venetian merchants were as familiar with
the Black Sea as the Adriatic; her ambassadors were to be
found in Isfahan and in Cairo; her travelers, stimulated by the
stories of Marco Polo, reached Sumatra and Ceylon long before
Vasco da Gama rounded the Cape. And even though the Venetians never ventured to such far-flung places as the Genoese at
the height of their greatness, their contacts with the East were
more stable, more secure, and made up in volume for what
they might lack in diversity.

By 1450 Venice was the only power in Italy, save for the
Papacy, that was truly cosmopolitan, one whose interests required not only a great fleet but also a complex intelligence
system. Venice needed to know the intentions of the Shah of
Persia, the Count of Flanders, the Sultan of Cairo, the King
of France, or the Duke of Ferrara. And every merchant, every
priest was expected to spy for his country's good. The Signory
knew at once the deepest secrets of the most carefully guarded
conclaves of the Papacy, for the patriarchs of Venice put loyalty
to the state higher than the command of the Church. The carefully, beautifully written, well-informed, judicious reports of
the Venetian residents in London, Paris, or Bruges now form
some of the most reliable sources not only for the history of
Venice, but also for the history of England, France, and the
Netherlands. In the great building of the Archivio Centrale,
next to the Frari church, is the greatest collection of archives
ever accumulated by a single city. There are a quarter of a
million books, documents, and parchments, which if placed
end to end would circle the earth eleven times. For the fourteenth and fifteenth centuries there is a multitude of papers, a
plethora of facts, a pyramid of accounts, still awaiting the toil
of the historian. The reason for it all lies in the attitude and

methods of the famous, or infamous, Council of Ten who, throughout the Renaissance, were the absolute rulers of the most highly organized state west of Byzantium.

The Council of Ten believed in knowledge; in facts: nothing was too trivial, too remote. They were as interested in the words and actions of a shopkeeper in the Campo di Santa Maria Formosa as in the gossip of the harem at Samarkand. So voracious was their desire to pry that, throughout Venice, they set up the famous Lions' Mouths by which Venetians could inform the Council anonymously of their suspicions of their neighbors. On this knowledge the Council acted swiftly and silently, for no public trials enlivened the Venetian scene, and there were no appeals. Once found guilty, the prisoner was sometimes quickly and efficiently strangled in the dungeons; or thrown into a part of the lagoon reserved for the purpose, where no fishing was allowed; or hanged by one leg from the pillars of the Doge's Palace; or quartered and distributed about the city; or buried upside down in the Piazzetta, legs protruding; or beheaded—as a public spectacle—between the great pillars on which stand Saint Theodore with his crocodile and the winged lion of Saint Mark. That was how the great condottiere Carmagnola met his end, when the Council discovered that he was prepared to sell Venice to her enemies. But most traitors went silently in the night, their broken bodies sending a shiver of horror through the waking city as dawn gilded the palaces and churches.

This formidable engine of government ruled with equal efficiency all departments of the state—finance, diplomacy, the navy, the army, the welfare of the city—and it would tolerate no real rivals. In the last resort the safety of the state, for which the Ten were responsible, overrode all other considerations. The powers of the Doge had been so ruthlessly suppressed (he could not even display his own armorial bearings) that he had become a mere ceremonial idol—a figure for pageants and

formal acts of state. The Church, too, bowed to the state. No
bishop, no parish priest, could officiate in Venice unless Venetian born. When placed under the Interdict by Pope Sixtus IV,
the Patriarch fell discreetly ill, and the Council told the clergy
that they would treat as a traitor any priest who refused to
celebrate the offices of the Church. The clergy ignored the Interdict. During the most savage years of the Counter Reformation, the Council protected the historian Sarpi, whom good
Catholics regarded as little better than a Lutheran. In Venice
there were no divided powers. Its immense wealth and its colossal maritime power were ruled with the iron will of a modern
dictatorship. Unbridled capitalism might flourish on the Rialto,
but the Doges' Palace was close cousin to the Kremlin.

The Council of Ten did not consist of permanent rulers. Its
powers, if not its final authority, were partly shared by the Col-
legio or Cabinet; and beyond these there was a more numerous
body still—the Senate or Signory from which the councils were
appointed. No one, however, by a decree of 1297, could sit on
these bodies unless his ancestor had been a member of the
Great Council between 1172 and 1297. In 1319, in order to make
certain that the purity of this oligarchy should be maintained,
the heraldic officers of the republic drew up the famous Golden
Book, the *Libro d'Oro,* 'as a perpetual studbook of Venice's
aristocracy. This revolution, for it was nothing less, deprived
the mass of Venetians of all the political rights they had possessed. The murmurs and rebellions against it were quickly and
ruthlessly suppressed, and, by the Renaissance, the patrician
families of Venice were as secure in their political and social
power as the English aristocracy of the eighteenth century. A
patrician's life was not, however, one of gilded leisure. The
aristocrats were expected to officer the fleets; trade was not regarded as ignoble; and the far-flung Venetian possessions required patricians for their government. Like the guardians of
Plato's republic or the proconsuls of British India, these men

were expected to lead lives dedicated to the state. Power and prestige might be theirs, but undeviating loyalty, exemplary courage, and unflagging generosity were the price they paid. If they aspired to the Doge's throne, they were aware of the risks, the dungeons, and the strangler's silent visit; if they sought glory in battle, their spirit was steeled by the grim epics of Venice's history—Admiral Dandolo, who bashed out his brains against the timbers of his galley the night the Genoese defeated him, or the neatly folded skin of Admiral Bragadino, flayed from his living body by a sportive pasha. Such is the dulcet beauty of Venice, with its time-eroded buildings swathed in the opalescent light of the lagoon, that it is all too easy to forget the stern, unyielding, harsh, and dedicated spirit that inspired its rulers in their days of greatness.

Venice, however, was Janus-faced. Her commerce might be regimented, her aristocracy disciplined and controlled, her people subjected, yet she was cosmopolitan as no other city in Europe was. The crowded wharves of the Rialto and the Riva degli Schiavoni saw Gentile and Jew, Moslem and Greek, haggling over rich caroges from the Orient. The Germans possessed a vast warehouse—decorated with frescoes by Giorgione—on the Grand Canal; the Turks, another, which had been the palace of the Pesaro family. Venice possessed the earliest ghetto in Europe, and the Armenians followed their religion for centuries without fear of the Inquisition. All the nations of Europe mingled with the races of the Near East. They were brought together by the simple fact that Venice was the greatest market of the Western world. Anything could be bought and sold in Venice, but the principal commerce was in luxuries—in spices, slaves, gold, silver, glass, silks, damasks, jewels—cargoes that were small in bulk but huge in worth. Throughout the barbarian times, when Venice grew to greatness, Europe lacked the sophisticated skills and crafts that were commonplace in the Eastern Empire, or in Syria and Egypt; and in return for products from these places, Venice could offer the cheap raw materials that a primitive Europe produced—hides and tin from England, fine cloth from Flanders, raw silver from Bohemia, copper and steel from Germany. And there were the pilgrims. Decade after decade, century after century, in peace or in war, rich and devout Christians won their way to heaven via the Holy Places, to the great profit of the Venetians. For centuries the Crusaders warred in the eastern lands, and the Crusaders paid; paid for themselves, their armies, their horses, their necessities—and Venetians did not believe in bargains. In spite of their great wars—against the Genoese, the Greeks, the Turks— Venice waxed rich: rich on man's craving for luxury, for ostentation, for self-indulgence, on the pride of life and the lust of the eye. All the skills that she encouraged were luxury crafts rather than industries. The glass manufacture of Murano, based on secrets learned in the East, was guarded by the Council of Ten: for any workman with the knowledge of its manufacture to leave Venice was an act of treason. The Council hunted him down and killed him. Along with the monopoly in glass went another—the making of mosaic: this art, derived from Byzantium, was practiced only in Venice. Venetian jewelers had no rivals in the late Middle Ages, and emperors and kings sent there for their crosses and scepters. Few Italian cities could rival Venice in the splendor of its silks, and none in the beauty of its lace. In Venice everything was for sale—love along with the rest. She boasted more courtesans than Rome. Their charges were carefully catalogued, and they were incomparable in skill as in price. They, too, had their rivals; the competition from homosexuals was so severe that the harlots complained loudly to the Council of Ten. As the wealth and prosperity of Europe lifted, so the riches of Venice soared.

On the threshold of the Renaissance, Venice possessed an unrivaled trade, and a stable and immensely powerful government firmly in the hands of its patricians. It was a city of hatchet-faced merchants. Jacopo Loredan entered in his great ledger: "The Doge Foscari: my debtor for the death of my father and uncle." After Foscari had been harried to death and his son killed, Loredan wrote on the opposite page, "Paid." In 1450 that was the spirit of Venice. By 1550 a gentler, softer, more self-indulgent atmosphere had turned Venice to a city of carnival: still strong, still rich, still capable of sacrifice, but essentially an empire in defense, wishing for a secure isolation in which to enjoy her immoderate riches. And this change was brought about partly through a change in strategy—itself the result of the growth of the Renaissance state—and partly through the spirit of the Renaissance itself.

Safe in the security of the lagoon, the strategic problems of Venice had been largely distant and maritime. Her diplomacy had been directed solely to the pursuit of trade, and the acquisition of territory had been subordinate to these ends. Throughout the High Middle Ages the Venetians had excluded themselves from Italy (sometimes they hinted that they owed an allegiance not to the West but to the Greek Emperor at Byzantium), but when it suited their purpose they forgot the East and made a token gesture to the Emperor of the West. So successful had this policy been that many influential doges and patricians regarded it as the foundation of Venice's glory. They felt that any deviation would ruin the state, and the deviation that they most feared was that the government would succumb to those who demanded that Venice should extend her frontiers on the mainland and take her place as a great power in Lombardy. The problem was one that all expanding commercial empires were to face: Did the needs of commerce require the political control of its channels? So long as the plain of Lombardy was divided up between a multitude of petty powers, Venice had little to fear, but in the fourteenth century the dominant powers in northern Italy became fewer and fewer, and the danger of their enmity was brought home

to the Venetians when Carrara, the despot of Padua, joined
with the Genoese in the war that Venice saved on the very
threshold of defeat by winning the great battle of Chioggia in
the lagoon itself. The safety of the lagoon, let alone Venetian
trade, depended upon the control of the great rivers—the
Brenta and the Piave—that had cost the republic huge sums
to canalize and divert from the lagoon. Beyond the rivers were
the easy Alpine passes, particularly the Brenner, through which
Venetian trade flowed to Northern Europe. And there were
subtler motives at work—everywhere in Italy small city-states
were going down like ninepins through the onslaught of Milan,
Florence, Rome, Naples, and if the Venetians wished to be
heard in the councils of Italy, they needed to acquire far more
Italian territory than a few muddy islands and river mouths
in a shallow lagoon. Finally, after the defeat of Genoa and
before the collapse of Constantinople, Venice had plenty of
money and plenty of young aristocrats ready for a venture.

Although the debate, particularly at the time of Doge Foscari, seemed bitter and prolonged, Venice was drawn inevitably
into the vortex of Italian politics and war. Once embroiled,
strategic needs forced her to push her frontiers ever westward
and southward against Milan and Rome. Her vicissitudes were
many, but her successes built up like a coral reef which, no
matter how frequently it is submerged, continues to grow.
There were years of danger, particularly when Venice struggled
singlehandedly to keep the Turks confined to the eastern
Mediterranean; there were even darker days when all the
princes of Italy combined with her enemies in the League of
Cambrai to ruin her. But Venice triumphed. Her frontiers
stretched from Lake Como in the west to Trieste in the east,
from the high Alpine valleys in the north to Ferrara in the
south. And these rich territories were ruled with wisdom and
restraint. No local customs were violated, no local law abro-
gated, no families uprooted. About all that the republic did

there was a hardheaded, bourgeois realism. The possession of Verona, Vicenza, Padua, Bergamo, Brescia, Treviso, and the rest added enormously to Venetian wealth in spite of the cost of the wars their capture entailed.

The patricians found they could tap the riches of the *terraferma,* as they called the Lombard plain, far more easily than they could the Oriental trade, rich as it was. The Turks were in Constantinople, and the frequent, costly, and bloody struggles that resulted made eastern trade more difficult and more uncertain than it had been in the time of the Greek emperors. That trade had always entailed risks, from pirates, shipwreck, or the hazards of the sea, but money in farms on the rich alluvial plains of the mainland brought in a high, steady return. In addition, there were choice opportunities in the captured towns —real estate, banking, insurance, partnerships in trade and industry—yet it was the land that attracted the Venetians. For centuries their rich families had built their villas and landscaped their gardens on the Giudecca and Murano. There, in the summer evenings, they had escaped from the heat and stink of Venice for their *fêtes champêtres*; for the music and dalliance that are so brilliantly portrayed by Giorgione and Titian. But tenements and warehouses crept along the Giudecca; Murano was eaten up by the ever-expanding glass works, so the lovely sweeping curves and gentle slopes of the valley of the Brenta or the wilder hills of Cadore drew the Venetian aristocracy to the rustic but sophisticated life of the countryside. There Palladio built the most exquisite villas in the Western world, villas that were to inspire the architects not only of eighteenth-century England, but also the planters of Virginia. Their walls were painted by Veronese and by Tiepolo; their owners' portraits by Titian or Tintoretto. Here they created an indulgent Arcadian life that stood in harsh contrast to the battle-scarred days of Venice's heroic growth. As ever, the strength of merchants was sapped by the delight in being landed gentlemen.

The same spirit was at work in Venice itself; the city had become stuffed and bloated with possessions. Although it proved tenacious, still, in clinging to what it had, it grew ever more indifferent to adventure. No Venetian galleys probed the secrets of the New World; no hardheaded merchants sought gold in tropical Africa. Perhaps it is not surprising that the early, exploratory, heroic phase of the Renaissance passed Venice by. Only, as it were, when the market in Renaissance goods was established did Venice enter it, but then she did so with a panache and a brilliance all her own. And furthermore, her proud independence and her utter indifference to the ideological strife of the sixteenth century enabled the spirit of the Renaissance to flourish long after it had been strangled elsewhere in Italy. Venetians, by the very nature of their experience in life, were quick to adopt technical improvements or to exploit the commercial possibilities of artistic development. The Flemish discovery in oil painting was quickly adopted by Venetian artists; the market for bronzes after the antique was flooded by Venetian craftsmen; family portraiture was a commonplace in Venice while it was unusual elsewhere. Whenever the calculating eye of the Venetian entrepreneur saw a main chance, he seized it. Printing, scoffed at in Rome and patronized in Milan, rapidly became a luxury industry with a growing mass market in the capable hands of Aldus Manutius and his family. The famous Aldine Classics were the first comprehensive, standardized sets of books produced. They lacked the beauty and rich ornamentation of the earlier books that attempted to ape the illuminated manuscripts, but about the Aldine Classics there is a spare and efficient functionalism. Elegant, not ornate, moderate in price, and easy to read, they were all that a book should be. Yet this was but one of over two hundred presses in Venice in 1500. Here the new printing trade, carefully nurtured and protected by the state, flourished as nowhere else.

Venice exploited with exceptional skill the bourgeois delights from which a growing public of increasing affluence derived intense satisfaction. Indeed, as her political and military power gently, almost imperceptibly, ebbed, she became the symbol of self-indulgence and sensuous living—a city of extravagance, urbanity, and sophistication, an aristocratic Bohemia in which the future was forgotten in the day's delights. In the end, bereft of all but the pageantry of power, the Venetians, as hardheaded as ever, plucked their profits from the gaping provincial nobility of Western and Northern Europe. But between 1450 and 1570, the great years of the Renaissance in Venice, there was still vigor enough in Venetian commerce, achievement enough in Venetian arms, to create legitimate pride. The lords of Venice could still live in an aura of greatness without any sense of falsity. Yet the weakening, the softening, was spreading everywhere as decade followed decade, like the growth of self-indulgent fat on an old warrior. This atmosphere of transition was exceptionally fertile for Venetian art, even though it sapped its power.

The Signory had always believed in the value of art as propaganda. They were willing to pay high prices for huge frescoes in the Doge's Palace that celebrated the heroic deeds of the republic or the noble acts of its great men. Indeed, after the doges died, they might be willing to immortalize them in a splendid portrait. And when it came to a pageant, their hard fists opened willingly. They delighted in parading the might and splendor of the republic. Saints' days, the acquisition of a new relic, the anniversaries of notable victories, the solemnization of treaties, the visits of monarchs and princes, the presentation and dismissal of ambassadors—all provided opportunities for glorious display, a kaleidoscope of color in which the costumes of the senators were as glorious as those of the ecclesiastics. As they wound their way through the Piazza, or in and out of the Doge's Palace, the powerless populace became visually aware of the greatness of their masters. It was a lesson, the Signory thought, that could not be learned too often—and they commanded Venice's outstanding artists to immortalize their pageants in paint and to embellish the walls of the Doge's Palace with the glories of the republic. Powerful guilds and rich patricians, with that quick eye for an opportunity, followed suit —and the life stories of Venice's favored saints in a peculiarly Venetian setting covered the charity schools and hospitals, the churches and monasteries of the city. Skilled craftsmen and painters had always been in demand in Venice, and the great personalities of Venetian art—the Bellini family, Giorgione, Titian, Carpaccio, Tintoretto, and Paolo Veronese—were surrounded by traditions that went back to the early Middle Ages. In Venice, because demand had been so heavy and the commissions so large, painting had to be a family affair, a workshop, almost a factory. The properties used for backgrounds were handed down generation after generation, some of Giovanni Bellini's reappearing in canvases a hundred years later. Every great Venetian painter was something more than an individual artist at work; he was the director and inspiring genius of a studio of painters in which brothers, wives, sons, daughters, journeymen, and apprentices all worked together. Naturally, this increased output, and it enabled a painter like Tintoretto to cover acres of wall and roods of canvas in his long and active life; so, too, was it easy for the Bellini and Titian to produce hundreds of portraits and scores of pictures of pageants and religious mythology. Venetian art exists in abundance; indeed, in Venice the feast is almost surfeiting— every church, every monastery swarms with masterpieces. This abundance, this astonishing fertility, reflects the three strands in Venetian life, its vigor, its wealth, and its sensuous delight. Of all painting of Renaissance Italy, the Venetian is most alive to color, to the warm sensuous delight in flesh and clothes and landscape played upon by light and shade. The Venetian master could move with consummate ease from painting a vast wall glorifying the state to the representation of the intimate enjoyment of physical love, yet whatever he might be painting there was warmth, and the reality that the Venetian knew. The huge *Paradise* of Tintoretto, the largest painting of its age, was peopled with Venetians. In Gentile Bellini's *Miracle of the Cross,* the canals, the gondolas, the roof tops and chimneys of Venice are all there. In Carpaccio's *Saint Ursula,* a Venetian girl sleeps in her bedroom; under the thin guise of a Christian story the rich, sensuous life pulsates, reflecting the splendor of the city.

Although the life of Venice was glorified in this way, individual men were not. An occasional doge, when dead, a patriarch or two, a brilliant condottiere, might be immortalized in a superb portrait or a statue—but the majority of portraits by Bellini or Titian have lost the names of their sitters, for they adorned the walls of those ordinary patricians who had no place in history—only the luck to be born in Venice at a time of artistic greatness. Yet how evocative are these portraits, how infinite their variety, and how sharp the sense of the transience of living and loving men that broods over them. Nostalgia emanates from things Venetian like miasma from the lagoon; the streets of Venice echo with a sense of loss. The poetry of existence, the sadness that veils a sensual life, informs not only the best Venetian painting but also the writing of its one outstanding literary genius—Aretino. In him were mirrored the conflicting images of man—the cosmic and the noble, the moral and the obscene—that were to hypnotize the creative writers of Europe for generations.

Venice at the crossroads of her destiny created a society of exceptional complexity. It was still the city of hardheaded merchants, still the city of enterprise and ingenuity, still the city of the all-pervading, all-powerful state, of the swift and terrible justice. Its claim to dominion over the sea did not ring hollow: the hieratic splendor of the Doge had not been reduced to a

quaint old-fashioned pageant. Yet the Renaissance settled on
Venice like a golden haze, sweetening life, softening the edges.
Venice had lost the future; from the city of commerce she was
becoming the city of carnival. And this feeling of the future
lost was already pervading much of the attitude to life of Venetian men and women, drawing them to the luxurious life which
they could so easily afford, to the new delights in painting,
music, architecture, and letters that the Renaissance produced
in such abundance. Rome itself could scarcely vie with Venice
in the splendor of its new buildings both public and private.
The splendid façades of Sansovino had given the Piazzetta its
permanent face, and scattered about the canals and islands of
the lagoon were the churches and monasteries of Palladio. Its
artistic luxuries were incomparable (so many craftsmen possessing such an ancient tradition were bound to throw up
genius after genius in the visual arts), and its gold and silver,
armor, jewelry, bronzes, glass, lace, printing, and bookbinding
—indeed all the arts and crafts that adorn the life of man—
were practiced not only with the highest skill but also in a
profusion that made Venice, both in its lagoon and on the mainland, the most affluent state of Italy. The splendor of its new
palaces of white marble, porphyry, and serpentine overwhelmed
generations of foreigners, while the profusion of its merchan-
dise bewildered them. Philippe de Comines, nobleman of
France, ambassador of its King, rich, sophisticated, much traveled, was as entranced by the Grand Canal—*"la plus belle rue
que je croy qui soit en tout le monde, et la mieulx maisonnée"*
—as the merry, uncouth joker Thomas Coryate of Somerset,
who walked all the way there and gaped, openmouthed with
amazement, believing himself in paradise. Other cities might
possess nobler paintings, statues, buildings; the spirit of the
Renaissance maintained in Florence a more heroic aspect, in
Rome its expression was more grandiose. But nowhere did it
permeate more thoroughly the daily life of a city and its people
than in Venice.

VIII

THE IMAGES OF
MAN

Venice, Rome, Milan, and Florence were, physically speaking, new cities—cities in construction littered with scaffolding, scarred with half-realized plans. The villas, the taverns, the lounging places in the piazzas and gardens were filled with earnest argument about the new cathedrals and palaces. The statues that adorn the Piazza della Signoria at Florence gleamed with an almost raw whiteness. The Piazza San Marco at Venice shook itself free from the clutter of stalls, bakers' shops, and latrines to acquire the beauty that we see. In Milan the new citadel of the Sforza drew a wondering crowd of enthusiasts. In Mantua, Parma, Naples, Perugia, Viterbo, Genoa, indeed in all the towns of Italy, it was the same story—a new physical world was being built that buried or obscured the old barbarisms. In the churches and monasteries scarcely a year passed without a new masterpiece being painted on the walls. Today the blackened surface and faded pigments baffle the imagination and make it difficult to recapture the sharp impact that these pictures had on the eyes that first saw them, and the same is true of statues and bronzes staled by centuries of reproduction and plagiarism. Impossible, too, to recapture the novelty of books, the miracle that it must have seemed to scholars to possess their own Virgil, their own Cicero, or to see their own poems and plays and familiar letters stacked by the hundreds in printers' shops. To this fresh, lavish, and splendid world were being added new horizons, and old certainties were dissolving as rapidly as the old scenes. Stories from Portugal and Spain, tales from Genoese sea captains, the gossip of the Venetian Cabots, told of a wondrous world of continents before undreamed of. Soon speculation became certainty, and the fables of Marco Polo and Mandeville gave way to the sober statements of mariners. The discoveries of Columbus, of the Cabots, of a whole generation of Portuguese in the Eastern Seas—"such great adventures as Fate had to no former age allowed"—confirmed the belief, already held by many men and women, that the age to which they belonged was original and new, and that the immediate past was dead. Undoubtedly such convictions bred a sense of liberation and encouraged a belief in the unique quality of personal destiny. Men began to create new images of themselves—a habit as old as man himself, but always fresh and entrancing.

"Men," wrote Alberti, "are themselves the source of their own fortune and misfortune." "O supreme generosity of God the Father," apostrophized Pico della Mirandola, "O highest and marvelous felicity of man. To him it is granted to have whatever he chooses, to be whatever he wills." Man was heroic, destined by his own nature to greatness or to failure, but eternally alone, eternally himself. If born wise, then he might of course benefit by the wisdom of the past; if sensitive, he would gain from philosophy and religion; if apt, he could acquire the education of a gentleman. In the last resort, however, all rested on himself—on his nature and on his luck, that curious personal destiny, controlled of course by God, but a mystery that could never be unlocked except by time. Portents and the conjunction or combustion of the stars might, as in a riddle, hint an answer, but essentially man was alone with fate. This attitude was deeply bound up with the growing capitalism of society, in which the merchant sought a profit by gambling on his own ingenuity, but there lay between these ideas a barrier of unawareness, like that which lies between the unconscious drives of a man's personality and his rational self. To the men who lived in the fifteenth century, this view of man—his individuality, his lonely destiny, his isolation—had nothing whatsoever to do with the active world or its expanding horizons. For them it was a new truth, self-evident, eternal, inescapable. As this attitude to man gathered momentum, it spread to places and communities that were unripe for its reception. Also it became entangled in the strong, clinging, wayward tendrils of the past. Men were still priests, monks, scholars, soldiers, aristocrats, and merchants, and each profession, each community, each class possessed rules, regulations, beliefs, and attitudes already centuries old. On these the new conception of man worked, but, in working, suffered its own sea change.

Yet the concept of man, untrammeled, as a creature of destiny, but with his destiny provoked by his own self, enthralled most of the sensitive spirits of the Renaissance. Its fascination is beautifully illustrated in the growth and development of drama and the theater. Plays there had been in medieval Europe, but they were a looking glass of morality, not a mirror of man. They had concerned themselves, often in an intensely human way, with God, Christ, the Virgin, with the Creation or the Flood, or with personified moralities—vices like Lust and Sloth, virtues like Chastity and Humility. The humanists and their circle found these plays barbarous. They took delight in Plautus and in Terence, in the obscenities and the jokes, the brave declamations and fateful tragedies of individual men and women, crude as they were, two-dimensional as they might now seem; to us they are caricatures rather than living men, yet the change from the immediate past was very great. So, too, in history, the humanists looked for heroes, not men, looked for the individual life lived on a scale of intensity and drama beyond the range and experience of common mortals. And this spirit spread through literature like a dye. All aspects of a personal life—birth, love, marriage, ambition, defeat, senility —were blown up, endowed with an excess that in the hands of a genius, a Tasso or an Ariosto, acquired a heroic and universal significance. If the dramatists, poets, rhetoricians, and novelists were often second rate, if their creations now seem bombastic and ridiculous, they entranced their contemporaries. Nothing was more fashionable at any court than plays, masques, the declamation of set speeches, the recitation of poetry, or even the reading of familiar letters between humanists. Of course, these fashionable literary banquets were concerned with more than the heroic nature of man. They provided a setting for the display of ancient learning, for the parade of the esoteric, for the language of concealment that all literary coteries delight in cultivating. And they also gave an opportunity for display—a physical setting was required, and all Renaissance man's delight in ostentation and sumptuous adornment was given full rein. The masques, poetic entertainments, and dances were produced regardless of cost; the drama itself created its own special theater, with scenery as spectacular and as realistic as the world was ever to know. Yet overlaid as the setting might be with a distracting luxury, time and time again the theme of poem or play or philosophic oration harked back to the lonely plight of man, to his capacity for heroism and for tragedy. Sometimes this was threaded with comic realism, with the sense of man's absurdity; at other times a portrayal of his vigorous instinctive life flashed over both the comedy and the tragedy. But always the writers were drawn back, as indeed were the painters and sculptors, to man—enlarged, ennobled, romanticized.

This attitude toward man did not remain merely a theme for the arts; it spread into society, modifying customs, penetrating politics and changing them. The belief—often unconsciously adopted—that man's instincts and abilities must find their own destiny, be it what it may, influenced sexual practices more profoundly than any other social conventions. In the

Middle Ages there had been sinners galore, priests, cardinals, popes who could not resist the itch of concupiscence; novices had been thrust into monasteries at too hectic a period of their adolescence; nuns found that the time of waiting for their heavenly groom lay heavily on their hands. And the laity, as ever, found the desires of the flesh pushing them through the barriers of accepted morality. But in the Middle Ages these things were wicked, a matter for penance and sorrow, matters to be suppressed and eradicated. A wandering scholar might glorify the sins of his flesh in a lyric, but medieval society condemned them. Not so in the Renaissance. Sex was par excellence the expression of the individual man. Nor were the humanists confined by Christian or Hebraic morality: they had read their Plato; they knew of the lives and loves of the gods. Jove had his Ganymede, why could not they? So Aeneas Silvius sends his bastard to his mother and father so they will have something of him to love. Pietro Aretino asks the Duke of Mantua to send him a boy that struck his fancy. Lorenzo Valla spends the leisure from his exacting scholarship in the Vatican library writing some of the most brilliant, and certainly the most obscene, familiar letters, a literary activity which Machiavelli, too, enjoyed with relish. The follies of Alexander VI provided no more gossip for Rome than did the follies of Arentino in his old age for Venice. Not since the days of Petronius had public men indulged themselves in such unmeasured erotic fantasy.

Untrammeled by convention, dominated by instinct, swept along by his nature, fulfilling his fate with the agility of an acrobat, yet true to his inner essence, his mysterious *virtù*—this was the compulsive image which Renaissance man created for himself. Instead of the stage being the mirror of life, it seemed rather as if the characters of melodrama had usurped the true characters of men. In no other man of this age is the image more sharply mirrored than in Pietro Aretino—the first Bohemian.

"I am a free man," Aretino wrote, "I do not need to copy

Petrarch or Boccaccio. My own genius is enough. Let others worry themselves about style and so cease to be themselves. Without a master, without a model, without a guide, without artifice, I go to work and earn my living, my well-being, and my fame. What do I need more? With a goose quill and a few sheets of paper I mock the universe." And he did, riotously, splendidly, until in his vigorous sixties he roared too vehemently at a bawdy joke, had apoplexy, and died. But what a life he had lived—shameless, selfish, magnificently free from humbug and splendidly creative.

Born the legitimate son of a poor shoemaker of Arezzo, Aretino passed himself off as the bastard of a gentleman until a fellow citizen, in a moment of rage, blew the *gaffe*; then Aretino boasted the truth as vehemently as he had paraded the lie. He received no serious education. He turned up for a time, in his late adolescence, at Perugia, probably living as a painter's apprentice. Already he had started to scribble sonnets. He next appears in the household of the great Roman banker Agostino Chigi (as a domestic servant, his enemies said, who was quickly dismissed for pinching the silver). Aretino claimed Chigi, however, as patron, not master. Whatever his situation, Chigi's household gave him a lifelong taste for luxury, feasting, and pomp. Rome also offered him a golden opportunity for his natural literary genius.

At the corner of the Piazza Navona, a worn antique statue had become a curious sort of notice board. Learned lampoons of the Pope's government and the leading personalities of Rome were stuck to it. It was called Pasquino after a bitter-tongued schoolmaster. Later another statue in the Campus Martius was used in a similar way, and then the two statues took to having dialogues. These were known as pasquinades. Most of them were dull and pedantic, but risky in a mild way because of the freedom of their criticism. Aretino changed all that—his opportunity came on the death of Pope Leo X. To press the claims of his candidate, Cardinal Medici, afterward Clement VII, Aretino launched a series of unbridled lampoons against the cardinals. Every vice they may have practiced (and Aretino's imagination was rich), every dishonorable event in their own lives or their families', was widely and mercilessly pilloried. To make it worse, these verses were printed and sold as handbills. Rome rocked with laughter; princes asked their ambassadors for copies. No one believed that such impudence could go unpunished, but it did. Aretino demonstrated the power of the pen; he became the "scourge of princes." However, when an old Dutchman was elected Pope, Aretino thought he would cool his heels in Mantua. There the Gonzaga enjoyed his talents and boasted of his presence at their court, but with the election of Cardinal Medici as Clement VII, Aretino was summoned back to Rome to regale the papal court with his wit and license. At Rome he began to write his superb comedy *La Cortigiana;* of course in Italian, and with complete disregard for the models of Terence and Plautus that were thought sacrosanct. His reputation for wit and daring soared to new heights. His fancy, however, became powerfully stimulated by sixteen remarkably obscene drawings by Giulio Romano that an enterprising publisher was about to have engraved. For each, Aretino provided a sonnet as explicit and as indecent as the picture. This did not endear him to his patron the Pope, who lacked the temperament and interests of the Borgia. At the same time Aretino was cuckolding as many husbands as he could. After a bad brawl in which he was nearly killed by an irate husband, the Pope's protection abruptly ceased. So off went Aretino to join the famous condottiere Giovanni delle Bande Nere. In that great captain, Aretino saw a mirror image—a man compelled like himself to follow his star, to fulfill his own life on his own terms, outside society, beyond custom, a man of destiny. With Giovanni he rejoiced in the freedom of military life, whose sweetness and pain were heightened by the dark presence of death. For a man of Aretino's powerful imagination and strong instincts, the grandeurs and miseries of war proved deeply enriching. The death of Giovanni acted as a traumatic experience which Aretino described in one of the most remarkable letters that he ever wrote. In it he depicted, in language that was simple, grave, and noble, the last hours of a heroic man, triumphing over pain, accepting death, making his own terms with God as he had done with man. After Giovanni's death, Aretino felt more keenly his isolation from society; in his bitterness he poured his acid scorn on popes and princes. However, he had to live, and with his usual journalistic flair he brought out an almanac in which he flayed men and affairs by predicting the year's events. Its vast success enabled Aretino to settle in Venice—free, secure, rich from his pen: princes tumbled over themselves either to obtain a few flattering lines of prose from him or to avoid mention altogether; even the Pope forgave and pampered him; everything he wrote sold handsomely. He lived like a prince on the Grand Canal, his *palazzo* full of women and boys—the Aretines, he called them. There he offered profuse hospitality, gargantuan banquets and feasts of love, orgies of literary gossip. Titian was drawn to him like a moth to a candle. He painted him over and over again, and in return Aretino pushed Titian's paintings on his patrons. They drank together, rioted together, lived the Bohemian life of the writer and artist that became one of the most seductive and compelling images of man, at once creative and destructive, and one that still had the power to hypnotize long after they were dead. Aretino's life gave great impetus to the idea that the artist was beyond morality, outside society, a spirit dedicated only to the compulsive needs of his art. At the same time he invested this image with a nobility, a certain grandeur, and the possibility of tragedy. The end of a free man could be brutal, harsh, and black with pain; in the midst of a riotous life those shadows were with him. Titian saw them in his face, and painted them.

Of course there were men who were alarmed by Aretino, shocked by his life, disgusted by his writings, who condemned him roundly. Christian morality and the precepts of the Church were to the majority of men not shackles on the instinctive life but principles by which it should be lived. Yet in spite of themselves many were drawn to the image that Aretino or men like him presented. And some were honest enough to admit it. True, they tended, like Machiavelli, to discover man as a free agent more in princes and in captains of war, in the life of decision and action, than in writers and the writers' life. In war and politics, if anywhere, man was solitary, alone, without friends, and of necessity, they believed, without principle. To survive, to succeed, to kill before being killed, such were their destined lives. And this image artists evoked in painting as Machiavelli did in prose; the profiles, the faces of the Renaissance princes, have a terrible majesty, an aloofness, a dedication beyond the reality of common men.

So complex a society, of course, created many images that expressed its needs and hopes and aspirations, and not all mirrored egotism and the pursuit of fame. To some, Aretino or Cellini with his "Men like Benvenuto . . . stand above the Law" were tedious. Men yearn to belong, to be secure, to be accepted. At a time when the courtly graces were being practiced in London, Paris, Dijon, or Avignon, the rocky fortresses of Urbino, Rimini, or Orvieto were full of raw robber barons, uncouth, scarcely literate. Few despots could boast a long ancestry: within a mere three generations the Sforza rose from peasants to princes; even the Medici had modest origins. Rich Italy might become, but many of its prosperous men felt insecure in the luxury they could afford. Yet there existed for them antique patterns of behavior. The knights of the late Middle Ages had developed chivalry into a code of manners, a complex dance of love as intricate as a tarantula's; Greece and Rome offered guides to gentility and sophistication. Above all there was Plato to teach them the efficacy of education; human nature, they hopefully believed, could be molded to what men might desire it to be.

This attitude was formulated most effectively by two men —Vittorino da Feltre, who ran an academy for boys and girls at Mantua, and Baldassare Castiglione, who became the arbiter of taste for the western world. Education, they both maintained, was more than learning: it was breeding, which might give what the heritage of blood had conferred on the nobles of the Middle Ages. Those knights had been required to learn the manners as well as the skills of the warrior's trade, to be "a verray parfit gentil knight," but the training did not confer *gentility*. That they inherited or, more rarely, won on the field of battle. The men of the Renaissance were concerned, however, to turn sow's ears into silk purses, peasants into princes.

The rough soldier of fortune and the uncouth merchant from the counting house wished to appear as men of breeding, as connoisseurs of taste, as representatives of antique virtue. Even though they spurned the fortune of birth, cared not a rap for legitimacy, they could not bear to be considered barbarous. Barbarity was shown in a man's deportment, in his attitude to women, in his pleasures, and, of course, in his possessions. Some things were easier to eradicate than others. Giovanni della Casa thought no perfect gentleman would thrust stinking fish under the noses of his friends, or closely examine the contents of his handkerchief, or sit so that the more intimate parts of his person were revealed, or pick his nose, or spit, or break wind. The fact that della Casa found it necessary to expatiate on such things in his handbook of gentlemanly behavior indicates the rudeness, the roughness, and the untutored nature of much of Renaissance society. But della Casa wanted more than behavior free from physical offense. He also stressed that no man could be a gentleman without modesty, without being "very desirous of beautiful things, well-proportioned and comely," and squeamish of all that was not. To achieve this, Vittorino da Feltre and his imitators thought that all activities of the child should be directed to that end. Gentility, they maintained, was not an attribute of correct conversation or well-chosen clothes; on the contrary, it was the whole being of man; indeed, the highest perfection a man could achieve was to be immediately recognized as a gentleman.

The qualities of soul, the aspects of refinement and sensibility, which marked off the perfect gentleman were, of course, subject to endless debate, in which the classics were ransacked for precepts. Vittorino established a certain canon of requirements: the body as well as the soul needed to be brought to perfection. Exercise, quickness of eye, control of the muscles, and grace of movement were linked to moral qualities which the proper use of the body promoted—courage, hardiness, stamina, indifference to pain and discomfort. Intellectual exercises, like physical ones, were aimed at building character, developing moral qualities, and for this purpose classical antiquities and mathematical knowledge had special merits: the former was full of the most excellent precepts, the latter revealed the harmonies of man and nature. Although many of the qualities which Vittorino sought in his pupils had been qualities of knightly perfection in earlier times, his attitude to boys and girls and to their educational needs was nearer far to Plato than to Aristotle. Above all, he believed that a gentleman should be literate and his aesthetic senses refined by teaching. Nor did he believe gentility to be conferred by birth; he educated the poor with the rich.

With the growing leisure and the growing secularization of life in the Renaissance, social pleasures became a pursuit in themselves. As ever with an emerging class, opulent but insecure, many yearned for the aristocratic distinctions of a previous age—long genealogies, emblazoned arms, the somewhat archaic extravagance of the joust and tourney. Some humanists, however, would have none of this hankering after the trappings of feudal nobility. "The longer the line of bold miscreants," wrote Poggio, "from which a man traces his descent, the further he is removed from true nobility." For him nobility lay in the individual heart and cultivated mind, in a man's nature and education—not in his birth. There was endless debate—snobbery, a desire for exclusiveness, drawing one way; a pride in the freshness and strength of their own world and times pulling another. In drawing rooms of courts, in the lounging places of the piazzas, in tents on the battlefield, in the country houses of bankers, men discussed over and over again the nature of men and the way of perfection. Or they argued on how they should act in love or in war, or what attributes they should cultivate, or which passions they should despise and suppress. Naturally men arose who became by common consent arbiters of such matters, and the greatest of these was certainly Baldassare Castiglione, who was, as might be expected, the son of an ancient, noble, but very poor family, a man whose birth drew him toward the old, but who lacked any future except with the new and emerging world of his own time.

His long, grave, handsome face with its expression of almost careless elegance became the image of what an aristocrat and a gentleman should look like. Everyone—kings as well as commoners—immediately recognized his quality. His presence at court was eagerly sought, and he conferred immortality on Urbino by writing of the conversations about the nature of a gentleman in which he had participated under the aegis of its blue-stocking Duchess. And in his *Book of the Courtier* there is portrayed another image of Renaissance man, distinct from Aretino's man of destiny; for Castiglione's man was a social being.

Belonging though he did to the knightly class, Castiglione was open-minded about birth. It was better to be born noble, easier to become a true gentleman if one were, but it was not, he reluctantly conceded, essential. Knightly virtues were, however, a necessity, for fighting, the pursuit of arms, the cult of honor, were the life of action to which a gentleman must dedicate himself. So courage and strength were prime virtues, and the exercise of the body a necessity. Horsemanship, fencing, wrestling, swimming, tennis—all things which gave the body suppleness and grace and power were proper pursuits for a gentleman. Naturally he must excel, but should avoid seeming to do so; above all he must cultivate grace of movement, and this Castiglione thought could only be achieved by the practice of *sprezzatura*, nonchalance, "so as to conceal all art and make whatever is done and said appear to be without effort and without almost any thought about it." Polish was as necessary as prowess, in exercises of the mind as well as the body. The gentleman was, of course, literate, knowledgeable about the classics, and eloquent. Learning must be lightly, negligently worn. Of course he should be quick in conversation but never thrusting, amusing but never mocking, humorous but never coarse, learned but never pedantic. And he must avoid being precious: eschew archaisms, never fear to use accepted colloquial speech, nor even bits of French and Spanish if they were in use in the society he frequented.

After the mind and the body came sensibility, connoisseurship. According to Castiglione, a gentleman might even be taught to paint—as, indeed, the Greek and Roman aristocrats had been. Music and its appreciation were necessities: music composed the mind, directed thought to gentle pleasures, inculcated a love of harmony. Music was essentially *right*. The lighter expressions of art as well as the weightier were proper pastimes—dances, masques, the parade of rhetoric, and, naturally, the pursuit of love (love, however, not lust). The conquest of the heart, the possession of the mind, were a courtier's targets: the consolations of lesser delights were not altogether to be despised, even though they were improper subjects for conversation. A certain hypocrisy made for social ease.

About all activities, from the discussion of philosophy to the tilt of a hat, there must be ease, grace, and nonchalance; nobility must shine through. The princes of Italy might be murderers, adulterers, traitors, violators of boys and girls, but Castiglione depicted them as they desired themselves to be, just as Titian painted them as they wished to look—distinguished, set apart by their *virtù* and destiny from other men, yet full of ease, grace, nobility, and charm. The image created by Castiglione and his imitators, for his book enjoyed a vast success, increased the civility of Italians, made their courts a byword for sophisticated living. The cleanliness of their homes, the decorum at their tables, the beauty of their clothes and furnishings, the elegance of their manners, became models for the rude provincial gentry of the northern countries. Indeed for many generations Italy became an obsession for the less sophisticated nations of Europe, for it provided Europe not only with images of men, but also with a mirage of aristocratic and courtly life. Of course between image and reality there was frequently enough of a chasm. Most men could not live like Castiglione. Crude manners, vulgar habits, coarse pleasures, the instinctive life of which Aretino sang, lurked even in the Courtier. The importance of Castiglione lies in the fact that men thought they *ought* to be like his Courtier, and valued men who seemed to achieve it.

In the High Renaissance, aristocratic attitudes triumphed over the rough bourgeois spirit of its earlier days. Certainly in so doing the idea of what an aristocrat should be suffered a profound change. The armed knight, chivalry itself, became, as in *Don Quixote*, a pathetic joke. Much of the world in which the new aristocracy moved with such elegance grew, after all, out of the activity of merchants, bankers, and seafarers, not out of feudalism. But the code of manners which evolved was not a merchant's code; it had little to do with the traditional attitudes of the middle class. By 1530 much that Alberti had written about the family in the fifteenth century wore an old-fashioned air, and lives devoted to the pursuit of gain were regarded as vulgar. Castiglione and others like him had helped to define the terms by which men were included in or excluded from gentility. It was essentially a private world with its own scale of values, but one that twinkled with recognition symbols. Style in the turn of a phrase or the cut of a cloak; fields of knowledge, of taste, even of sport, that a gentleman might know or practice; attitudes to love, to religion, to the prince—all these things marked off the gentleman from the man. The rich could achieve this exclusive world only by leaving the countinghouse behind and getting away from the rattle of the loom.

This, as we shall see, had profound consequences, and still has, for Western society. But the importance of the dominating image of man created by the Renaissance lies in this: it arose after the heroic age of Italy's commercial and industrial expansion was past. It belonged to the gilded twilight world of a luxurious but defeated society—defeated not only by the discoveries of the outer world which had given Western Europe the future, but also by the exceptional resilience of its traditional class structure which triumphed over the pragmatism, the disorder, the violent economic and political changes, of Renaissance Italy.

It was against this world of Castiglione—a society at once charming, elegant, inbred, and effete—that Aretino and his followers had to rebel, and so present the image of a genius for which conventions are but naught. Castiglione taught men how to belong, Aretino how to live.

IX

WOMEN
OF THE RENAISSANCE

François Villon, the vagabond poet of France, wondered, as he drifted through the gutters and attics of fifteenth-century Paris, where were the famous women of the days long past? Where Héloïse, for whom Abelard had endured such degradation? Where Thaïs, Alis, Haremburgis, where the Queen Blanche with her siren's voice, where were these fabled, love-haunted, noble women, of more than human beauty? Gone, he thought, gone forever. Even the rough Viking bards sang of their heroic women, of Aud the Deep-minded who "hurt most whom she loved best." The lives of these fateful, tragic women, medieval heroines of love and sorrow, became themes of epic and romance which were told in the courts of princes; yet even as Villon bewailed their loss, men were growing tired of them.

The age of heroes was dying. The unrequited love of Dante for Beatrice, the lyrical attachment of Petrarch for Laura, and, in a different mood, the agreeable pleasantries of Boccaccio, had domesticated love, making it more intimate. The dawn of a care-free, less fate-ridden attitude to woman was gentle, undramatic, and slow, beginning way back with the wandering troubadours and scholars who moved from castle to farm, from monastery to university, singing their light-hearted lyrics to earn their keep.

> *Down the broad way do I go,*
> *Young and unregretting,*

127

Wrap me in my vices up,
Virtue all forgetting,
Greedier for all delight
Than heaven to enter in:
Since the soul in me is dead,
Better save the skin.

Sit you down amid the fire,
Will the fire not burn you?
Come to Pavia, will you
Just as chaste return you?
Pavia, where Beauty draws
Youth with finger-tips,
Youth entangled in her eyes,
Ravished with her lips.

So sang the nameless Archpoet, young, consumptive, in love, as he wandered down to Salerno to read medicine. The time was the twelfth century—three hundred years before the haunting love poems of Lorenzo de' Medici were written. Yet the sentiments of both men were a part of the same process, part of the lifting tide of Southern Europe's prosperity, of its growing population, of the sophistication that wealth and leisure brought: for in leisure lies dalliance. The wandering of scholars were few; their mistresses, chatelaines or girls of the town: yet they were the naïve harbingers of a world that was to reach its fullness in Italy in the fifteenth century.

It was the new prosperity that influenced the lives of women most profoundly. It brought them fresh opportunities for adornment; it increased their dowries and their value. It emancipated many from the drudgery of the household and from the relentless, time-consuming demands of children. Women entered more fully into the daily lives and pursuits of men. And, of course, the new delights of the Renaissance world—painting, music, literature—had their feminine expression. Much of the artistic world was concerned with the pursuit of love in all its guises. Women were a part of art.

Except for the very lowest ranks of society, women were inextricably entangled in the concept of prosperity, and their virtue was a marketable commodity. They were secluded from birth to marriage, taught by women and priests, kept constantly under the closest supervision in the home or in the convent. Marriage came early: twelve was not an uncommon age, thirteen usual, fifteen was getting late, and an unmarried girl of sixteen or seventeen was a catastrophe. Women conveyed property and could often secure a lift in the social scale for their families. Even more important was the use of women to seal alliances between families, whether princely, noble, or mercantile. The great Venetian merchants interlocked their adventures overseas with judicious marriages at home. The redoubtable Vittoria Colonna was bethrothed at the age of four to the Marquis of Pescara to satisfy her family's political ambition. Lucrezia Borgia's early life was a grim enough reminder of the dynastic value of women. Her fiancés were sent packing, her husbands murdered or declared impotent, so that Alexander VI could use her again and again in the furtherance of his policies. In less exalted ranks of society women were still traded. It took Michelangelo years of horse-trading to buy a young Ridolfi wife for his nephew and so push his family up a rank in Florentine society. Marriages so arranged were symbolic of power and social status as well as of wealth, and their celebration, in consequence, demanded the utmost pomp and splendor that the contracting parties could afford. Important Venetian marriages were famed for an extravagance that not even the Council of Ten could curb. The festivities began with an official proclamation in the Doge's Palace. The contracting parties and their supporters paraded the canals *en fête*. Gondoliers and servants were dressed in sumptuous livery; the façades of the palaces were adorned with rare

Oriental carpets and tapestries; there were bonfires, fireworks, balls, masques, banquets, and everywhere and at all times—even the most intimate—serenades by gorgeously dressed musicians. Of course, such profusion acted like a magnet for poets, dramatists, rhetoricians, painters, and artists of every variety. For a few ducats a wandering humanist would pour out a few thousand words, full of recondite references to gods and heroes; poets churned out epithalamiums before they could be asked; and painters immortalized the bride, her groom, or even, as Botticelli did, the wedding breakfast. And they were eager for more mundane tasks, not for one moment despising an offer to decorate the elaborate *cassoni* in which the bride took her clothes and linen to her new household. Indeed, the competitive spirit of both brides and painters in *cassoni* became so fierce that they ceased to be objects of utility and were transformed into extravagant works of art, becoming the heirlooms of future generations.

The artistic accompaniment of marriage became the height of fashion. When the Duke and Duchess of Urbino returned to their capital after their wedding, they were met on a hilltop outside their city by all the women and children of rank, exquisitely and expensively dressed, bearing olive branches in their hands. As the Duke and Duchess reached them, mounted choristers accompanied by nymphs *à la Grecque* burst into song— a special cantata which had been composed for the newlyweds. The Goddess of Mirth appeared in person with her court, and to make everyone realize that jollity and horseplay were never out of place at a wedding, hares were loosed in the crowd. This drove the dogs insane with excitement, to everyone's delight. No matter how solemn the occasion, marriage always involved coarse farce, usually at the climax of the wedding festivities, when the bride and groom were publicly bedded. Although there was no romantic nonsense about Italian weddings, certainly few marriages for love, everyone knew that the right true end of the contract was the bed. The dowager Duchess of Urbino, something of a bluestocking and a Platonist, and a woman of acknowledged refinement, burst into her niece's bedroom on the morning after her marriage and shouted, "Isn't it a fine thing to sleep with the men?"

Marriage for the women of the Renaissance gave many their first taste of opulence, leisure, and freedom. They were very young, the atmosphere of their world was as reckless as it was ostentatious and, furthermore, they had not chosen their husbands, who frequently were a generation older than themselves. Their men, who were usually soldiers or courtiers who lived close to the razor edge of life, fully enjoyed intrigue, so the young wife became a quarry to be hunted. As she was often neglected, the chase could be brief. Even Castiglione, who was very fond of his wife, treated her somewhat casually. He saw her rarely, and made up for his absence with affectionate, bantering letters. Of course, she was a generation younger than himself and therefore hardly a companion. Such a situation was not unusual: a girl of thirteen might excite her mature husband, but she was unlikely to entertain him for long. She fulfilled her tasks by bearing a few children and running a trouble-free household, and neither matter was too onerous for the rich. Nurses took over the children as soon as they were born; a regiment of servants relieved wives of their traditional housewifely duties. So the leisure which had previously been the lot of only a few women of very high birth became a commonplace of existence for a multitude of women.

The presence of these leisured women in society helped to transform it. It created the opportunity for personality to flourish, for women to indulge the whims of their temperaments—free from the constraining circumstances of child birth, nursery, and kitchen. There were men enough to adorn their vacant hours. Italy was alive with priests, many of them urbane, cultured, and idle, whose habit acted as a passport, hinting a security for husbands which their actions all too frequently belied. Nevertheless, they were the natural courtiers of lonely wives, and they swarmed in the literary salons of such distinguished women as Elisabetta Gonzaga at Urbino, the Queen of Cyprus at Asolo, or Vittoria Colonna at Rome. Soldiers as well as priests needed the sweetness of feminine compassion to soften their tough and dangerous lives. Fortunately, military campaigns in Renaissance Italy were short and usually confined to the summer months, and so the horseplay, the practical jokes, and the feats of arms which were as essential to the courtly life as literary conversations or dramatic performances were provided by the knights. In addition to soldiers and priests, there were the husbands' pages, all in need of the finer points of amorous education. For a princess, further adornment of the salon was provided by an ambassador —often, true enough, a mere Italian, but at times French or Spanish, which gave an exotic touch that a woman of fashion could exploit to her rivals' disadvantage. Naturally, these courts became highly competitive: to have Pietro Bembo sitting at one's feet, reading his mellifluous but tedious essays on the beauties of Platonic love, was sure to enrage the hearts of other women. In fact, the popularity of Bembo illustrates admirably the style of sophisticated love that the extravagant and princely women of Italy demanded.

Pietro Bembo was a Venetian nobleman, the cultivated son of a rich and sophisticated father who had educated him in the height of humanist fashion at the University of Ferrara, where he acquired extreme agility in bandying about the high-flown concepts of that strange mixture of Platonism and Christianity which was the hallmark of the exquisite. Petrarch, of course, was Bembo's mentor, and like Petrarch he lived his life, as far as the pressures of nature would allow him, in literary terms. He fell verbosely and unhappily in love with a Venetian girl; his ardent longings and intolerable frustrations were committed elegantly to paper and circulated to his admiring friends. This experience provided him with enough material for a long epistolary exchange with Ercole Strozzi, who was as addicted as Bembo to girls in literary dress. Enraptured by the elegance of his sentiments, Strozzi invited Bembo to his villa near Ferrara, doubtless to flaunt his latest capture, Lucrezia Borgia, as well as to indulge his insatiable literary appetite. However, the biter was quickly bitten, for Bembo was just Lucrezia's cup of tea. A mature woman of twenty-two, thoroughly versed in the language as well as the experience of love, she was already bored with her husband, Alfonso d'Este, and tired of Strozzi. Soon she and Bembo were exchanging charming Spanish love lyrics and far larger homilies on aesthetics. After a visit by Lucrezia to Bembo, sick with fever, the pace quickened. Enormous letters followed thick and fast. Bembo ransacked literature to do homage to Lucrezia; they were Aeneas and Dido, Tristan and Iseult, Lancelot and Guinevere—not, however, lover and mistress. For a time they lived near each other in the country, while Ferrara was plague-ridden. Proximity and the furor of literary passion began to kindle fires in Bembo that were not entirely Platonic, and, after all, Lucrezia was a Borgia. Her tolerant but watchful husband, however, had no intention of being cuckolded by an aesthete, and he rattled his sword. Bembo did not relish reliving the tragedy of Abelard; he might love Lucrezia to distraction, but he cherished himself as only an artist can, so he thought it discreet to return to Venice (he had excuse enough, as his brother was desperately sick). There he consoled himself by polishing his dialogue, *Gli Asolani*, which already enjoyed a high reputation among those to whom it had been circulated in manuscript. Resolving to give his love for Lucrezia its final, immortal form, he decided to publish it with a long dedication to her. To present her with his divine thoughts on love was a greater gift by far, of course, than his person. Doubtless both Lucrezia and her husband agreed; whether they read further than the dedication is more doubtful.

Bembo had written these highfalutin' letters—informal, mannered, obscure, and so loaded with spiritual effusions on love, beauty, God, and women that they are almost unreadable—during a visit to that tragic and noble woman Caterina Cornaro, Queen of Cyprus. The daughter of a Venetian aristocrat, she had been married as a girl to Giacomo II of Cyprus for reasons of state and declared with infinite pomp "daughter of the republic." Bereaved of both husband and son within three years, she had defied revolution and civil war and maintained her government for fourteen years until, to ease its political necessities, Venice had forced her abdication and set her up in a musical-comedy court at Asolo. There she consoled herself with the world of the spirit, about which Bembo was better informed than most, and he was drawn to her like a moth to a candle. Her court was elegant, fashionable, and intensely literary. *Gli Asolani*, published by Aldus in 1505, made Bembo the archpriest of love as the *Courtier* was to make Castiglione the archpriest of manners. Indeed, Bembo figures in the *Courtier*, and Castiglione adopted his literary techniques. These two subtle and scented bores were destined to turn up together, and nowhere was more likely than the court of Elisabetta Gonzaga at Urbino, for her insatiable appetite for discussion was equal to their eloquence; her stamina matched their verbosity; and night after night the dawn overtook their relentless arguments about the spiritual nature of love. Neither, of course, was so stupid as to think that even the high-minded Caterina or Elisabetta could live by words alone, and Bembo, at least, always interlarded the more ethereal descriptions of Platonic love with a warm eulogy of passion in its more prosaic and energetic aspects. Indeed, he was not above appearing (not entirely modestly disguised) as an ambassador of Venus, in order to declaim in favor of natural love. After six years of this excessively cultured refinement at Urbino, Bembo became papal secretary to Leo X in Rome. Appropriately, at Rome the word became flesh, and Bembo settled into the comfortable arms of a girl called Morosina who promptly provided him with three children. It is not surprising, therefore, that Bembo's interests became more mundane, turning from Platonic philosophy to the history of Venice. After the death of his mistress, the life of the spirit once more claimed him, and he entered the College of Cardinals in 1538. More than any other man of his time, he set the pattern of elegant courtship, so that the flattery of the mind, combined with poetic effusions on the supremacy of the spirit, became a well-trodden path for the courtier. It possessed the supreme advantage of passionate courtship without the necessity of proof—a happy situation, indeed, when the object was both a bluestocking and a queen.

Even though the great ladies of Renaissance Italy cultivated the heart and mind so ardently, some of them did not wish to neglect entirely the more commonplace forms of love. They liked their flattery to be carnal, even though love was pure. They insisted on being admired for their physical charms, and they were prepared to listen, as Lucrezia Borgia was, to a lengthy eulogy not only about the charms of their spirit but also on the beauty of their dress, upon which they spent as profusely as any women in the history of mankind. The jewels of the Este girls at Ferrara came in for almost as much praise as their intellects. The extravagance of their fashions, like their predilection for poets, was eagerly imitated in less exalted circles. Blonde hair became so much *de rigueur* that a brunette was not to be seen in Venice except among the working classes. Venetian women spent hours dyeing and burnishing their hair until they achieved the harsh metallic glitter that was considered a necessity. But in these things the women of the Renaissance were no different from women of any age: the only change from the immediate past was that their wealth permitted them greater luxury, giving them greater opportunities of self-indulgence; and the fact that there were, at this time, more wealthy women than ever before meant that the jealous competition between them was intensified.

Yet it would be wrong to think that the gilded lives of Renaissance princesses were merely elegant, sophisticated, and luxurious, or that flirtation took place only in the most refined language. Few could concentrate their thoughts year in, year out, on the nobility of love like Vittoria Colonna. She, who inspired some of Michelangelo's most passionate poetry even as old age was ravaging her features, could and did live in an intense world of spiritual passion, in which the lusts of the flesh were exorcised by an ecstatic contemplation of the beauties of religion. The miracle was that she retained her charm, avoided the pitfalls of hypocrisy, and secured without effort the devotion of Castiglione and Bembo as well as Michelangelo. Even the old rogue Aretino attempted to secure her patronage, but naturally she remained aloof. In her the Platonic ideals of love and beauty mingled with the Christian virtues to the exclusion of all else. Amazingly, no one found her a bore. However, few women could live like Vittoria: they sighed as they read Bembo, became enrapt as they listened to Castiglione, but from time to time they enjoyed a quiet reading of Boccaccio and, better still, Bandello.

Matteo Bandello had been received as a Dominican and spent many years of his life at the Convento delle Grazie at Milan, which seems to have been a more exciting place for a short-story teller than might be imagined. He acted for a time as ambassador for the Bentivoglio and so came in contact with that remarkable woman Isabella d'Este Gonzaga, whose court at Mantua was as outstanding for its wit, elegance, and genius as any in Italy. There Bandello picked up a mistress, which put him in no mind to hurry back to his brother monks. At Mantua, too, he laid the foundations of his reputation for being one of the best raconteurs of scandal in all Italy, Aretino not excepted. How true Bandello's stories are is still a matter for fierce warfare among scholars, but this they agree on: they did not seem incredible to those who read them. That being so, they give a hair-raising picture of what was going on at courts, in monasteries, in nunneries, in merchant houses, in the palaces and parsonages of Italy. The

prime pursuit, in the vast majority of Bandello's stories, is the
conquest of women, and to achieve success any trick, any false-
hood, any force, is justifiable. His heroes' attitude to success in
sex was like Machiavelli's to politics—the end justifies any means.
The aim of all men is to ravish other men's wives and daughters
and preserve their own women or revenge them if they fail to
do so. Vendettas involving the most bloodcurdling punishments
are a corollary to his major theme. In consequence, Bandello's
stories, cast in a moral guise, nevertheless read like the chronicles
of a pornographer. Here are the themes of a few that were
thought to be proper entertainment for the lighter moments of
court life or for quiet reading by a bored wife—the marriage
of a man to a woman who was already his sister, and to his
daughter; the adultery of two ladies at a court and the death
of their paramours, which is a vivid record of sexual pleasure
and horrifying punishment; the servant who was decapitated
for sleeping with his mistress; the death through excessive sexual
indulgence of Charles of Navarre; Gian Maria Visconti's burial
of a live priest; the autocastration of Fra Filippo—and so one
might go on and on, for Bandello wrote hundreds of short
stories and they were largely variations on a single theme. The
women of the Renaissance loved them, and few storytellers were
as popular as Bandello (such abilities did not go unmarked, and
he finished his career as Bishop of Agen). Nor was Bandello
exceptional: there were scores of writers like him. Malicious,
distorted, exaggerated as these tales were, they were based on
the realities of Italian life. Undoubtedly the increased leisure of
men and women released their energies for a more riotous
indulgence of their sexual appetites.

However daring the Italian males of the Renaissance were,
the prudence of wives and the vigilance of husbands prevailed
more often than not. The Emilia Pías, Elisabetta Gonzagas, Isabella d'Estes, Lucrezia Borgias, Costanza Amarettas, and Vittoria
Colonnas were all too rare—particularly for cardinals and bishops

ravenous for Platonic love. So in Rome, in Florence, in Venice, and in Milan there developed a class of grand courtesans, more akin to geisha girls than to prostitutes, to the extent that the *cortesane famose* of Venice despised the *cortesane de la minor sorte* and complained of their number, habits and prices to the Senate (they felt they brought disrepute on an honorable profession). Grand as these Venetian girls were, they could not compete with the great courtesans of Rome, who not only lived in small palaces with retinues of maids and liveried servants, but also practiced the literary graces and argued as learnedly as a Duchess of Urbino about the ideals of Platonic love. Imperia of Rome, for example, held a salon for priestly humanists and gratified their spiritual as well as their carnal lusts with a delicacy and grace that made her name legendary. Her virgin daughter had been brought up so immaculately that she even threatened suicide to escape the amorous advances of a randy cardinal. Such a quean did honor to Rome, and her death was celebrated as a day of public mourning.

Even Imperia, however, could scarcely hold a candle to Tullia d'Aragona, the authoress of *On the Infinity of Perfect Love*, a subject for which her profession, perhaps, gave her special insight. Certainly she drove the aesthetes crazy. She was rhapsodized on her arrival at Ferrara in June, 1537, in these terms: "There has just arrived here a very pretty lady, so staid in deportment, so fascinating in manner, that we cannot help finding in her something truly divine. She sings all sorts of airs and motets at sight; her conversation has matchless charm; she knows everything and there is nothing that you cannot talk to her about. There is no one here to hold a candle to her, not even the Marchioness of Pescara" (*i.e.*, Vittoria Colonna!). Tullia actually preferred her clients to be philosophers or historians. After Leo X had chased her and her sisters from Rome, she settled in Florence, where the reigning Duke insisted that all whores should wear yellow as a mark of their infamy. Her admirers, however, protested so vehemently on Tullia's behalf that she was publicly excused by the government on the grounds of "literary talents that are found in her to the great joy of noble minds."

Italy during the Renaissance was a country at war, plagued for decades with armies. A well-versed condottiere might battle with skill even in the wordy encounters of Platonic passion, but the majority wanted quicker and cheaper victory. For months on end the captains of war had nothing to do and money to spend; they needed a metropolis of pleasure and vice. Venice, with its quick eye for a profit, provided it and plucked them clean. There girls were to be had for as little as one *scudo*, well within the means even of a musketeer. And it was natural that after Leo X's purge, the majority of the fallen from Rome should flow to Venice. That city, with its regattas, *feste*, and carnivals, with its gondolas built for seclusion and sin, became a harlot's paradise. The trade in women became more profitable and extensive than it had been since the days of Imperial Rome. The Renaissance recaptured the past in more exotic fields than literature or the arts.

Life, however, for the noble women of the Renaissance was not always cakes and ale; it could be harsh and furious: the male world of war, assassination, and the pursuit of power frequently broke in upon their gentle world of love and dalliance. Indeed, Caterina Sforza, the woman whom all Italy saluted as its *prima donna*, won her fame through her dour courage and savage temper. Castiglione tells the story of the time she invited a boorish condottiere to dinner, and asked him first to dance and then to hear some music—both of which he declined on the grounds that they were not his business. "What is your business, then?" the hostess asked. "Fighting," the warrior replied. "Then," said the virago of Forlì, "since you are not at war and not needed to fight, it would be wise for you to have yourself well greased and put away in a cupboard with all your arms until you are wanted, so that you will not get more rusty than you are." Violent, sensual, inexhaustible, contemptuous, and credulous, she is more a figure of a saga than a woman of the Renaissance. Three of her husbands were assassinated. At one time she defied the French, at another Cesare Borgia, who caught her and sent her like a captive lioness to the dungeons of Sant' Angelo. She had told her frantic sons that she was habituated to grief and had no fear of it, and as they ought to have expected, she escaped. Yet tough and resourceful as she was, Caterina could be a fool in love—much more of a fool than the Duchess of Urbino or Vittoria Colonna. Time and time again her political troubles were due to her inability to check her strong sensual appetite, which fixed itself too readily on the more monstrous of Renaissance adventurers. So eventful a life induced credulity, and like the rest of her family, Caterina believed in the magical side of nature, dabbled in alchemy and mysteries, and was constantly experimenting with magnets that would produce family harmony, or universal salves, or celestial water, or any other improbable elixir that the wandering hucksters wished on her. At any age, at any time, Caterina would have been a remarkable woman, but the Renaissance allowed her wild temperament to riot.

Certainly the women of the Renaissance were portents. Elisabetta Gonzaga and Isabella d'Este are the founding sisters of the great literary salons that were to dominate the fashionable society of Western Europe for centuries. But the courts of Italy were few, the families that were rich enough to indulge the tastes and pleasures of sophisticated women never numerous. The lot of most women was harsh; they toiled in the home at their looms or in the fields alongside their men. They bred early and died young, untouched by the growing civility about them, save in their piety. In the churches where they sought ease for their sorrows, the Mother of God shone with a new radiance, a deeper compassion, and seemed in her person to immortalize their lost beauty. Even the majority of middle-class women knew little of luxury or literary elegance. Their lives were dedicated to their husbands and their children; their ambitions were limited to the provision of a proper social and domestic background for their husbands; and they were encouraged to exercise prudence, to indulge in piety, and to eschew vanities. Yet their lives possessed a civility, a modest elegance, that made a strong contrast to the harsher experiences and more laborious days of medieval women. Their new wealth permitted a greater, even if still modest, personal luxury. They could dress themselves more finely, acquire more jewels, provide a richer variety of food for their guests, entertain more lavishly, give more generously to charity. Although circumscribed, their lives were freer, their opportunities greater. It might still be unusual for a woman to be learned or to practice the arts, but it was neither rare nor exotic. And because they had more time, they were able to create a more active social life and to spread civility. After the Renaissance, the drawing room becomes an integral part of civilized living; indeed, the Renaissance education of a gentleman assumed that much of his life would be spent amusing women and moving them with words. As in so many aspects of life in Renaissance Italy, aristocratic attitudes of the High Middle Ages were adopted by the middle classes. Courtesy and civility spread downward, and the arts of chivalry became genteel.

X

THE SPREAD OF THE

RENAISSANCE

In the autumn of 1511, Erasmus, the most distinguished scholar of Northern Europe, took up his lodgings again in Queens' College, Cambridge—a cold, bleak room that overlooked the marshes of the fens. He was poor, he was frightened of the plague that raged about the University, he was very lonely. He had been swept to England by the tide of the Italian Renaissance, not for the first but for the third time. For five wearisome years Erasmus moldered in Cambridge until he could stand the poverty and the ignorance no longer, and off he went on his journeys again, to the Netherlands, to Switzerland, to Germany, always carrying with him the memory of those years in Italy when he had discovered himself. The new learning had filled him with such hope that not even the sorrows and hardships of his personal life could eradicate it. In 1517 he could still write, "Immortal God, what a world I see dawning! Why can I not grow young again?" Nor was Erasmus unique. In London one of the most gifted, yet wayward, of Florentine sculptors, Torrigiano, was modeling, under the soaring Gothic arches of Westminster Abbey, the first Renaissance tombs of Northern Europe, built to immortalize Heny VII and his wife, Elizabeth of York. For decades the currents created not only by cataclysmic events such as the invasion of Italy by the French kings, but also by the excitement of the new learning, had been drawing such men as

Erasmus and Torrigiano into or out of Italy. And that sense of wonder, of a new world and a new dawn of the spirit, touched less sensitive men than Erasmus. Henry VII conferred the Garter, the highest order of English chivalry, on the Duke of Urbino, and the court of Windsor witnessed the embassy of Castiglione who came to receive it for his master. So profound was Henry VII's respect for the Italian scholarship that he asked Polydore Vergil to write what became the first serious and dispassionate study of England's history. Indeed, the presence of Erasmus in England was due entirely to a devoted band of humanists—Linacre, Grocyn, and Colet—who had studied in Padua, Florence, and Rome, seeking to acquire facility in Greek and a knowledge of the old as well as the new philosophies. Their attitude was deeply Christian, and their aim was to perfect their theology through a more exact knowledge of the early Fathers. The employment of Pietro Torrigiano was also due to the same band of humanists, which included Lord Mountjoy as its patron and John Fisher as its chaplain, both of whom were intimately connected with the English royal family. What was true of England was also true of the Netherlands, of Germany, and of Spain.

As the Renaissance spread beyond the Alps, it was checked in Italy. In 1495 Charles VIII invaded Naples and in so doing unleashed thirty years of carnage. In the Lombard plain battle followed battle, draining away wealth, disrupting trade, heaping up taxes, destroying conditions favorable to art and learning. Furthermore, the riches of the New World, so recently discovered, poured into Spain, the Netherlands, France, and England, but not into Italy; wealth went west, and with it art. And then came Luther, who in 1517 hammered his Protestant theses to the church door of Wittenberg. To hold off the Reformation, the Papacy needed a sterner spirit; the luxurious and wanton times of the Borgia and Medici were brought to an end, and a militant asceticism replaced the self-indulgence of Renaissance Rome. No wonder Vasari regarded the venerable Michel-angelo as a relic of the age of heroes. This lonely, solitary artist had become the symbol of a time that had passed.

By 1500 Italy exerted a hypnotic influence, and just as the princes of the Western world wished to acquire the services of Italy's great painters and sculptors, so, too, did the artists of this outer world feel themselves drawn to Italy. The great Flemish school of painters might be secure within its own great tradition and therefore possess little or no sense of inferiority when confronted with the brilliance of the Italian achievement; and in fact it contributed as much in technique and originality as it derived from Italy. The same was not true, however, of the French or the German artists. They had been ravished by the books of engravings of Italian pictures that had begun to circulate after 1470. Crude as these were, they sufficiently hinted the beauties of the masters they copied to excite an over-whelming curiosity. Albrecht Dürer, as a young apprentice at Nuremberg, somehow acquired engravings of Pollaiuolo and Mantegna. Already in a tentative, schoolboyish, and rather shocked manner he had begun to draw from the nude, but these engravings helped to release his spirit from the harsh, moral, and cruelly realistic treatment of naked women that had become traditional in Gothic Germany. Engravings were not enough, however, and try as he might the secret of the Italian painters seemed to elude him. He believed that the for-mula for successful painting of the human figure, like some ancient mystery, was kept hidden by Italian artists. He sought the magic formula in Italy itself, deepened his imagination, im-proved his technique, but never found what he sought, and to his death the Gothic tradition into which he had been born held him in thrall. Yet without his Italian experiences and without his preoccupation with Italian art, his own achievement would have been less noble. As with Dürer, so with scores of artists great or small over the next four hundred years. They came to Italy as on a pilgrimage, for here was the source of their art. The painting of El Greco is as idiosyncratic as any artist's of Western Europe, yet his art is indelibly stamped with the years that he spent in Venice. The way he draws, the glittering light that runs along the edge of his figures, derives from Tintoretto, as his color does from Titian. The two greatest French artists of the seventeenth century—Nicolas Poussin and Claude Lorraine—spent most of their working lives in Rome. Titian—his color, his atmosphere, even his figures—entranced Poussin. Again and again, artists of the highest genius—Velázquez, Rubens, Rembrandt, Goya, Renoir—paint the same themes, sometimes even copy the same pictures, that the artists of the Renaissance had first conceived and executed. Giorgione's reclining Venus haunts European painting like a dream. All who aspired to greatness in painting needed to make the long journey to Italy. Some, like Sir Joshua Reynolds, went in great comfort under the patronage of the rich; others, like Richard Wilson, went on foot and in poverty, painting for their bread. Until the twentieth century, the traditions created by the Italian Renaissance were those in which all Western European artists worked.

The French kings and their courtiers during their invasions of Italy were delighted by much that they saw in Milan and Venice: the Certosa of Pavia especially caught their imagination. On the other hand, the austere and more truly classical buildings of Florence left them unmoved. So at first Italian influences on the new luxurious hunting lodges that the French nobility were building along the Loire combined, as at Chambord, the basic plan of a traditional medieval castle with the sophisticated elevation and greater comfort of an Italian palace. For a time this marriage of the old and the new satisfied Western Europe, but in the end, no matter how much inspiration might twist and turn within its national traditions, or frolic in the riotous decoration of the Baroque, it was drawn back, time and time again, to the purity of classical achievement, to Brunelleschi, to Bramante, to Palladio, and, finally—just before the Gothic revival destroyed architectural taste throughout Western Europe—to the Greek. In the visual arts, in its themes as well as its techniques, the achievements of the Italian Renaissance permeated Europe like an indelible stain. They expressed the world in which men wished to live—their dreams, their aspirations, as well as their actualities.

The arts of the Renaissance were not the only achievements that seeded themselves throughout the countries of the Western world. Changes that had taken place in Italy generations earlier were happening in Western Europe in the sixteenth century, with the result that a similar sort of society grew up with similar needs. Its basis, like Italy's, was mercantile and urban; and it was ambivalent toward the old feudal nobilities —longing for their grace, their courtliness, and their sense of privileged destiny, yet hating their special rights, their selfish and jealous independence that could cut so savagely across the needs of society as a whole, to the detriment of trade and profit. The new men longed for professional government, for a powerful person who could secure order and inculcate into a barbarous and anarchic society the *civilitas* of the ancients. For them the fountain of this political knowledge was Italy: there the wisdom of the classical world, of Plato, of Aristotle, of Cicero, had been sifted and refined and adjusted to modern necessities. Even more importantly, the University of Padua could teach them the secrets of Roman government through the study of its laws. Again, the Italians had made a profession of diplomacy in Europe of the fifteenth century which had come to be regarded as essential to good government as statistical analysis is in the twentieth. Men of affairs in London, in Paris, in Brussels, in Madrid, in the towns and states of Germany, thought that they could only manage their new and baffling societies if they or their subordinates had studied in Italy. Most of Henry

VIII's ministers of state—Wolsey, More, and Thomas Crom-well—were fascinated by the new learning, and they encour-aged scholarship whenever they could. Wolsey endowed Christ Church, Oxford, in order to establish the study of the new humanities in England. Thomas More became the life-long friend of Erasmus. Cromwell lent his rare and precious Italian books to his friends and encouraged young men such as Thomas Starkey, who had spent years studying civil law at Padua in the household of Reginald Pole. (Pole, who was a Plantagenet and a kinsman of Henry VIII, maintained a small court of English scholars at the University of Padua.) This in-terest in Italian learning certainly had its practical aspects, but it captivated them all—even Cromwell, that hammer of the monasteries—at a deeper level than practical usefulness.

This new learning seemed to hold the secrets of life itself for most of them and, for the more sensitive, some of the secrets of eternity. More and his friends—Colet, Linacre, Grocyn—were deeply religious men. So were Lefèvre d'Étaples and his colleagues in Paris; so were Ulrich von Hutten and Reuchlin in Germany. They reverenced Italian scholarship, for it took them, via a knowledge of Greek, to the purest texts of the New Testament. Here, they felt, they would find a faith cleansed from the impurities and evasions created by centuries of com-ment and explanation. By applying the new skills of philology and textual criticism which the Italian humanists had perfected, they would, they hoped, lay bare Christianity in its purest and most historical form and thereby strengthen the Church. This attitude toward religion fused with another, equally serious, but Flemish rather than Italian in origin. Before Renaissance in-fluence had touched Northwestern Europe there had been a strong revival of religious mysticism, led by the Brethren of the Common Life, which had been given literary and devo-tional form by Thomas à Kempis in his *Imitation of Christ*. This mysticism stressed the importance of the individual's direct relation with God, and, by implication, lessened the importance of the priesthood and the Church. The search for historical truth, through scholarship, became linked with this search for truth in the exercise of the individual's religious conscience; and both became the seeding ground of Protestantism.

No one is more typical of the linkage between Italian humanism and reformed Christianity than Erasmus, who prepared the ground for Luther. A bastard son of a priest, half-tricked into monastic life, sensitive, excluded both by his habit and temperament from an active life of the instincts, he concentrated his heart and mind on friendship with scholars of like tastes. A man of formidable intellectual ability and exquisite literary gifts, his vast reputation was built up not only by personal contact and familiar letters, but also by the new invention of the printing press. His sharp satire—*The Praise of Folly*—exploited the sensationalism which only the press can give, and his Latin translation of the Greek Testament established his reputation as a scholar with a rapidity that no one could have achieved in earlier centuries. For Erasmus, the institutions of the Church and its learning were encrusted with silliness, stupidity, and barbarity. Christian faith could never regain its pristine clarity until this dross of centuries was cleared away. Yet he was no Protestant, no revolutionary, and he retreated rapidly from the position toward which Luther with his furious denunciations and precipitate actions seemed to be dragging him. Naturally he refused to listen to Albrecht Dürer's ardent plea: "O Erasmus of Rotterdam, where wilt thou tarry? . . . Hear, Christian knight, ride forth with the Lord Jesus . . . defend the right, obtain the martyr's crown!" He preferred to die in his bed: scared of the new age whose coming in 1517 he had welcomed with such joy. But for Dürer the reformation of religion was an inspiration greater and deeper than any experience of his life, greater even than his artistic experience in Italy.

Undoubtedly the scholars and critics had undermined, by their sharp attack on contemporary religious practices, the institutions of the Church; they mocked priests, bred resentment against papal taxation, and held the popes themselves up to the ridicule many deserved. Although some like Erasmus drew back, others such as Melanchthon and Peter Martyr, the Italian humanist, were prepared to go forward with Luther, feeling that he was leading them to the true dawn of a new age, to the rebirth of Christianity as Christ preached it. So the spirit of the Italian Renaissance, once it crossed the Alps, was diverted into new channels, plunging from the broad, sunlit meadows of secular delights into the dark ravines of religion.

Yet this political and religious twist to Italian influence was, for the early part of the sixteenth century, largely, if not entirely, confined to England, the Netherlands, and Germany. In France there were men like Erasmus, friends of his, deeply concerned with theology, deeply distrustful of scholasticism, as ardent as he was for pure religion. Yet they were not typical of French society as More and Colet or even Thomas Cromwell were typical of England. French society was more sophisticated, more secure, readier far to pursue that language of personal expression which lies at the heart of the Italian Renaissance. Much of Italian civilization—the gardens, the clothes, the furnishings and decoration of houses and places, the general civility of life, had entranced Philippe de Comines and many another noble Frenchman with the invading armies of Charles VIII and Louis XII. But it was Francis I who really fell in love with Italy and things Italian in spite of the fact that the greatest humiliation of his career—his defeat by the Emperor Charles V —took place at Pavia. He was the first prince outside Italy to begin a collection of paintings and sculpture by the great Italian masters. He persuaded Leonardo da Vinci to spend his last years at Amboise, close to his great hunting lodges at Blois and Chambord. He did everything he could to entice Michelangelo to live in France and nearly succeeded. (He had to be content with a *Hercules* his agent bought.) With Benvenuto Cellini he was more successful. This fabulous rogue, a boastful, swashbuckling liar, yet a craftsman of genius, entranced Francis, who tolerated his extravagance and forgave his bad temper for the sake of the embellishments (among them Cellini's superb gold saltcellar which is so justly famous) with which he was adorning his châteaux.

Francis I was not merely a collector; he wanted his court to outshine in literature and in manners, as well as in art, the most famous courts of Italy, and he flung his cloak of patronage on all who might bring distinction to his country. In this he was aided by his remarkable sister, Marguerite of Navarre, who can claim, perhaps, to be one of the most outstanding women of the Renaissance. She wrote the *Heptameron,* a bawdy collection of stories, after the style of Boccacio; a mystical tract called *The Mirror of the Sinful Soul,* and a number of outstanding spiritual hymns. She corresponded with Erasmus, befriended Protestants, was accused herself as a heretic by the Sorbonne, and patronized Rabelais. Her court contained the whole world of letters, as complex and as strange as her own temperament. Indeed, many of the contradictions in her own self-expression reflected the contradictions of French artistic and intellectual society as it struggled to assimilate the achievements of Italy not only with its own Gothic traditions but also with those new horizons—intellectual as well as geographical—which the great discoveries had disclosed to the Western world. For Italian humanists, discovery lay in the past, in the art and history of their ancestors or their country's ancestors, the Greeks. With Frenchmen and with Englishmen, discovery also meant new worlds that knew neither Christianity nor Christian government nor Christian morality. To men such as Rabelais, Montaigne, Marlowe, Shakespeare, or Bacon, insecurity, anxiety, and elation mingled haphazardly and fused into art. Reverence for the past, a yearning for the safety of tradition, alternated

with the intoxicating sense of the capacity of man, the uniqueness of his experience, and the splendor and freshness of the
world about him.

In Rabelais, the greatest writer of the French Renaissance,
this conflict was apparent both in his restless, troubled life and
in his writings. Like Erasmus, he was a rebel monk who hated
the ignorance and immorality of monastic life. He sought truth
in the world. "Abandon yourself," he wrote, "to Nature's
truths, and let nothing in this world be unknown to you."
Rabelais followed his own dictum and it led him to strange
places—to alchemy, to astrology, to the mysterious exoticism
which seemed to offer new truth in the intellectual chaos of
sixteenth-century Europe. And his great work *Gargantua and
Pantagruel* is as odd and as moving as Rabelais' own quest for
self-knowledge. Gargantua, Pantagruel, and Grangousier, the
chief characters of this extraordinary fantasia, have the twisted
extravagance of Gothic gargoyles. They are gross representatives of the instinctive life, yet full of satire and wisdom, capable
of nobility and understanding. Above all they are in search of
life and truth. And in the midst of their fantastic adventures
comes the description of the Abbey of Thelema, a Utopian
world that might have been dreamed by Castiglione. The
turmoil and confusion of real life is stilled by the contemplation
of realized ideals; men and women achieve the noble life. The
whole book is written in a fabulous style, by a man utterly
drunk with words. It is almost as if Rabelais had himself discovered language. This mixture of barbarity and civility, of
satire and sincerity, entranced the French court. The Church
might be scandalized, the Protestants outraged, but Pantagruel-
ism became chic, the fashion of the aristocracy. It was original,
it was in tune with the medley and confusion of contemporary
life, and above all, it was French.

As soon as a literary renaissance begins to flourish either in
France or in England or in Spain, a strong nationalist sentiment

rapidly infuses it, and the delight that writers and artists took in the Italian achievement led not only to emulation but also to envy. In 1549 Joachim du Bellay published his pamphlet *La Défense et illustration de la langue française* (cribbed almost entirely from Speroni's defense of Italian) in which he exhorted Frenchmen to challenge in their own language the triumphs of antiquity. The same court circle that patronized Rabelais took du Bellay's exhortation as a battle cry. Fortunately, du Bellay could practice what he preached. He and his friend Ronsard and their group, *La Pléiade,* produced excellent lyrics. They, too, were preoccupied with the loneliness of men and their dependence on love and affection to save them from unbearable solitude. In Marguerite of Navarre, Ronsard, Rabelais, du Bellay, and the rest, the court of Francis I possessed a galaxy of talent that would have been a credit to any court of Italy. Owing vast debts to the Italian Renaissance, they nevertheless achieved a style, an idiom, and a theme that were distinctly French.

The same was to be true of the great efflorescence of literature that took place in England shortly afterwards. Plots, characters, in fact entire plays were lifted wholesale from Italian authors. The intentions of Edmund Spenser would have drawn from Castiglione nothing but his entire approval, and Spenser's debt to Ariosto's *Orlando Furioso* is as obvious as it is large. Yet there is no plagiarism: all is transmuted, Englished. Like Rabelais, the Elizabethans grew drunk on the discovery of their language. At the same time they were even less confined by tradition than the French, and their sense of achievement was far sharper, for the English were closer in time to barbarity and to anarchy. The great promise of the days of Chaucer, Langland, and Wycliffe had been checked by the maelstrom of the fifteenth century. The Wars of the Roses had ripped apart the fabric of English life. The violent class turmoil of the early Tudor period which followed, which had led men of affairs to seek guidance in politics and diplomacy in Italy, had begun to settle by the reign of Elizabeth I into a new pattern of society in which gentlemen—but not noblemen—predominated. The break with the Church, combined with increasing knowledge of the worlds beyond Europe, intensified this sense of a new age, of an original time. Yet the very dissolution of the past created anxiety, insecurity, a sense of isolation, and a longing to discover standards. The dramatists held up a looking glass to this society in conflict. The violence, the rapacity, the passion of their age was more acceptable to the audience that thronged to see their plays if they were cast in Italy, in ancient Rome, or more daringly in their own historic past. For their crude audience, the crimes in the *Duchess of Malfi* or the *White Devil* possessed a further dimension of evil and horror if set in the criminal splendor of an Italian court where incest, riot, poison, and murder were, everyone believed, commonplaces of life. As well as stimulating the poetic imagination of a Webster or a Tourneur, however, Italy and its Renaissance still possessed a serious purpose for Englishmen. Long after politicians had given up expecting to find the secrets of their craft there, and long after dramatists had exhausted the plots of its authors, Italy continued to exert the deepest influence.

Profoundly important as the influence of the Italian Renaissance might be on art and literature and learning, it was greater still in education, using that word in its widest possible sense. This possessed two aspects—one for the narrow circle of intellectually creative men, the other for the world at large. How far the intellectual skepticism of the Renaissance, with its search for truth in the evidence presented by men and events rather than in dogma and authority, stimulated the growth of a rational attitude to the world is difficult to know. Certainly without the greater stimuli of the discovery of the world beyond Europe and the revolutionary achievements of science in the seventeenth century, it might easily have come to naught. However, to belittle the importance of those first broad cracks that were made in fifteenth-century Italy in the all-embracing dome of dogma is to falsify history. Ideologies were still to rage in the heart of man and haunt his destiny, but for Western man never again could there be two opposed worlds of Christians and heretics. Important though this impetus was to the habit of truth, to the growth of a scientific and skeptical spirit in the world of learning, it is of minor significance compared with the influence which the Italian Renaissance had on the social patterns which Western Europe adopted.

Italy, with Flanders, had been the first country in Europe to grow really rich on commerce, to throw up a middle class which could challenge the economic, political, and social power of the aristocracy. These merchants, bankers, craftsmen, found their first real security in economic life. This they knew; this they controlled. And so they organized their political and social life about their economic activity—in guilds—and ignored as far as they could the structure of the world about them. But the pressure of their wealth and the needs of their professions forced them from their exclusive habits, forced them into contact (and at times into conflict) with the aristocracy, whose sources of wealth, invigorated by the rise of commerce, remained large enough to maintain their privileged place in society. In the end a linkage was made between the aristocracy and the middle class: they remained distinct but joined by paths that men could traverse, and this mingling wrought a profound change in social customs, in manners, in education, in the images of man that seemed socially valuable. In its search for standards, Italy could look where the Flemish could not—into its highly sophisticated past, to the days of Rome and Greece when life had also been urban, rich, and aristocratic, yet commercially minded. Although antiquity could provide some ingredients, it could not provide all, and the merchants' hunger to belong drove them to accept readily many of the concepts of feudal aristocracy.

By 1530 or so, however, Italian society had brought into being an idea of a gentleman that was neither classical nor feudal, neither noble or bourgeois, neither rural nor urban, but a fusion of all of those. The projection of this image acquired such intensity because Western Europe had begun to undergo the same sort of violent social revolution that Italy had undergone between 1300 and 1450. In the sixteenth century commercial wealth poured into Cadiz, Lisbon, Bordeaux, Nantes, London, Antwerp, Hamburg. It raced through the veins of rural society, erupting, creating, destroying. The new men of this age—and there were thousands of them—felt great social insecurity. They had to learn to be gentlemen, to move at ease in the aristocratic world which they could not or would not eradicate. They adopted the pattern of compromise which the Italians had established. They wolfed down the courtesy books—della Casa as well as Castiglione. They adopted Italian clothes and Italian manners. They educated their children according to Italian precepts. A knowledge of a great deal of Latin and a little Greek became an absolute necessity for anyone who aspired to gentility, from the North Cape of Norway to the Strait of Gibraltar. And a gentleman was not only delineated by his education, he also required breeding—those aristocratic airs, that easy nonchalance, that assumption of privileged position lightly borne, which Castiglione had emphasized over and over again. A taste in the visual arts, or connoisseurship, was as essential a part of breeding as skill in sitting a horse. As Europe assimilated its vast wealth, and society became more ordered, so this image of a gentleman became more tenacious. It represented, as it did in Italy, the triumph of the aristocracy at the expense of the middle class, whose own merits—prudence, reticence, professional education—came to be regarded as either boorish or comic, from which the young not only wished to escape but were encouraged to do so. This is why the possession of land achieved such sanctity in Western Europe—it was the way to salvation, the route by which a merchant's children might become gentlemen and gentlewomen. Excluded from true social power, hypnotized by the snobbery and sophistication of aristocratic life to which the Italian Renaissance had given such vivid definition, the merchant classes of Europe lost much of their dynamic and creative energy, and it took nearly two centuries of frustration before they challenged, in the age of Napoleon, the aristocratic foundations of European society.

During this period from the Reformation to the French Revolution the spirit of the Italian Renaissance pervaded Europe. It taught the rough and very raw provincial aristocracies of the West how to live, how to move at ease through a world of bourgeois delights, without being contaminated by it. Certainly it intensified snobbery, hardened the stratification of classes of men, and checked the scientific imagination by insisting on the education of character rather than of aptitudes. In return it gave much. It taught the new men of Europe that the purpose of art, the call of learning, were an essential part of the use of wealth. And it projected a theme—the uniqueness of personal experience, the idea of man caught in the jaws of Time—that has given rise to the world's greatest art and literature. The spirit of the Italian Renaissance broods over these centuries which link the age of feudalism to modern times, and makes them a part of itself.

INDEX

Format by Lydia Link
Set in Linotype Granjon
Composed by V & M Typographical, Inc.
Printed by Murray Printing Company
Bound by The Colonial Press
HARPER & ROW, PUBLISHERS, INCORPORATED

Revised November, 1964

harper ☫ torchbooks

HUMANITIES AND SOCIAL SCIENCES

American Studies

JOHN R. ALDEN: The American Revolution, 1775-1783.† Illus. TB/3011

BERNARD BAILYN: The New England Merchants in the Seventeenth Century TB/1149

RAY STANNARD BAKER: Following the Color Line: American Negro Citizenship in the Progressive Era.† Illus. Edited by Dewey W. Grantham, Jr. TB/3053

RAY A. BILLINGTON: The Far Western Frontier, 1830-1860.† Illus. TB/3012

JOSEPH L. BLAU, Ed.: Cornerstones of Religious Freedom in America. Selected Basic Documents, Court Decisions and Public Statements. Revised and Enlarged Edition TB/118

RANDOLPH S. BOURNE: War and the Intellectuals: Collected Essays, 1915-1919.‡ Edited by Carl Resek TB/3043

A. RUSSELL BUCHANAN: The United States and World War II. † Illus. Vol. I TB/3044
  Vol. II TB/3045

ABRAHAM CAHAN: The Rise of David Levinsky: a novel. Introduction by John Higham TB/1028

JOSEPH CHARLES: The Origins of the American Party System TB/1049

THOMAS C. COCHRAN: The Inner Revolution: Essays on the Social Sciences in History TB/1140

T. C. COCHRAN & WILLIAM MILLER: The Age of Enterprise: A Social History of Industrial America TB/1054

EDWARD S. CORWIN: American Constitutional History: Essays edited by Alpheus T. Mason and Gerald Garvey TB/1136

FOSTER RHEA DULLES: America's Rise to World Power, 1898-1954.† Illus. TB/3021

W. A. DUNNING: Reconstruction, Political and Economic, 1865-1877 TB/1073

A. HUNTER DUPREE: Science in the Federal Government: A History of Policies and Activities to 1940 TB/573

CLEMENT EATON: The Freedom-of-Thought Struggle in the Old South. Revised Edition. Illus. TB/1150

CLEMENT EATON: The Growth of Southern Civilization, 1790-1860.† Illus. TB/3040

HAROLD U. FAULKNER: Politics, Reform and Expansion, 1890-1900.† Illus. TB/3020

LOUIS FILLER: The Crusade against Slavery, 1830-1860.† Illus. TB/3029

EDITORS OF FORTUNE: America in the Sixties: the Economy and the Society. 72 two-color charts TB/1015

DIXON RYAN FOX: The Decline of Aristocracy in the Politics of New York.‡ Edited by Robert V. Remini TB/3064

LAWRENCE HENRY GIPSON: The Coming of the Revolution, 1763-1775.† Illus. TB/3007

FRANCIS J. GRUND: Aristocracy in America: Jacksonian Democracy TB/1001

ALEXANDER HAMILTON: The Reports of Alexander Hamilton.‡ Edited by Jacob E. Cooke TB/3060

OSCAR HANDLIN, Editor: This Was America: As Recorded by European Travelers to the Western Shore in the Eighteenth, Nineteenth, and Twentieth Centuries. Illus. TB/1119

MARCUS LEE HANSEN: The Atlantic Migration: 1607-1860. Edited by Arthur M. Schlesinger, Sr.; Introduction by Oscar Handlin TB/1052

MARCUS LEE HANSEN: The Immigrant in American History. Edited with a Foreword by Arthur M. Schlesinger, Sr. TB/1120

JOHN D. HICKS: Republican Ascendancy, 1921-1933.† Illus. TB/3041

JOHN HIGHAM, Ed.: The Reconstruction of American History TB/1068

---

† The New American Nation Series, edited by Henry Steele Commager and Richard B. Morris.
‡ American Perspectives series, edited by Bernard Wishy and William E. Leuchtenburg.
* The Rise of Modern Europe series, edited by William L. Langer.
‖ Researches in the Social, Cultural, and Behavioral Sciences, edited by Benjamin Nelson.
§ The Library of Religion and Culture, edited by Benjamin Nelson.
Σ Harper Modern Science Series, edited by James R. Newman.
º Not for sale in Canada.

Anthropology & Sociology

History: Renaissance & Reformation

R. R. BOLGAR: The Classical Heritage and Its Benefici-
aries: *From the Carolingian Age to the End of the
Renaissance*   TB/1125

JACOB BURCKHARDT: The Civilization of the Renaissance in Italy. *Introduction by Benjamin Nelson
and Charles Trinkaus. Illus.*   Volume I TB/40
                                     Volume II TB/41

ERNST CASSIRER: The Individual and the Cosmos
in Renaissance Philosophy. *Translated with an Introduction by Mario Domandi*   TB/1097

EDWARD P. CHEYNEY: The Dawn of a New Era,
1250-1453.* *Illus.*   TB/3002

DESIDERIUS ERASMUS: Christian Humanism and
the Reformation: *Selected Writings. Edited and
translated by John C. Olin*   TB/1166

WALLACE K. FERGUSON et al.: Facets of the Renaissance   TB/1098

WALLACE K. FERGUSON et al.: The Renaissance: *Six
Essays. Illus.*   TB/1084

MYRON P. GILMORE: The World of Humanism, 1453-
1517.* *Illus.*   TB/3003

FRANCESCO GUICCIARDINI: Maxims and Reflec-
tions of a Renaissance Statesman: *Ricordi. Trans.
by Mario Domandi. Intro. by Nicolai Rubinstein*
                                                     TB/1160

JOHAN HUIZINGA: Erasmus and the Age of Reformation. *Illus.*   TB/19

ULRICH VON HUTTEN et al.: On the Eve of the
Reformation: *"Letters of Obscure Men." Introduction
by Hajo Holborn*   TB/1124

PAUL O. KRISTELLER: Renaissance Thought: *The
Classic, Scholastic, and Humanist Strains* TB/1048

PAUL O. KRISTELLER: Renaissance Thought II:
Papers on Humanism and the Arts   TB/1163

NICCOLÒ MACHIAVELLI: History of Florence and of
the Affairs of Italy: *from the earliest times to the
death of Lorenzo the Magnificent. Introduction by
Felix Gilbert*   TB/1027

ALFRED VON MARTIN: Sociology of the Renaissance.
Introduction by Wallace K. Ferguson   TB/1099

GARRETT MATTINGLY et al.: Renaissance Profiles.
Edited by J. H. Plumb   TB/1162

MILLARD MEISS: Painting in Florence and Siena after
the Black Death. *The Arts, Religion and Society in
the Mid-Fourteenth Century. 169 illus.*   TB/1148

J. E. NEALE: The Age of Catherine de Medici°   TB/1085

ERWIN PANOFSKY: Studies in Iconology: *Humanistic
Themes in the Art of the Renaissance. 180 illustrations*   TB/1077

J. H. PARRY: The Establishment of the European Hegemony: 1415-1715   TB/1045

HENRI PIRENNE: Early Democracies in the Low
Countries: *Urban Society and Political Conflict in the
Middle Ages and the Renaissance. Introduction by
John Mundy*   TB/1110

J. H. PLUMB: The Italian Renaissance: *A Concise
Survey of Its History and Culture*   TB/1161

FERDINAND SCHEVILL: The Medici. *Illus.*   TB/1010

FERDINAND SCHEVILL: Medieval and Renaissance
Florence. *Illus.* Volume I: *Medieval Florence* TB/1090
            Volume II: *The Coming of Human-
ism and the Age of the Medici*   TB/1091

G. M. TREVELYAN: England in the Age of Wycliffe,
1368-1520°   TB/1112

VESPASIANO: Renaissance Princes, Popes, and Prel-
ates: *The Vespasiano Memoirs: Lives of Illustrious
Men of the XVth Century. Introduction by Myron P.
Gilmore*   TB/1111

History: Modern European

FREDERICK B. ARTZ: Reaction and Revolution,
1815-1832.* *Illus.*   TB/3034

MAX BELOFF: The Age of Absolutism, 1660-1815
                                                     TB/1062

ROBERT C. BINKLEY: Realism and Nationalism, 1852-
1871.* *Illus.*   TB/3038

CRANE BRINTON: A Decade of Revolution, 1789-
1799.* *Illus.*   TB/3018

J. BRONOWSKI & BRUCE MAZLISH: The Western
Intellectual Tradition: *From Leonardo to Hegel*
                                                     TB/3001

GEOFFREY BRUUN: Europe and the French Imperium,
1799-1814.* *Illus.*   TB/3033

ALAN BULLOCK: Hitler, A Study in Tyranny.° *Illus.*
                                                     TB/1123

E. H. CARR: The Twenty Years' Crisis, 1919-1939: *An
Introduction to the Study of International Relations*°
                                                     TB/1122

GORDON A. CRAIG: From Bismarck to Adenauer:
Aspects of German Statecraft. Revised Edition
                                                     TB/1171

WALTER L. DORN: Competition for Empire, 1740-
1763.* *Illus.*   TB/3032

CARL J. FRIEDRICH: The Age of the Baroque, 1610-
1660.* *Illus.*   TB/3004

LEO GERSHOY: From Despotism to Revolution, 1763-
1789.* *Illus.*   TB/3017

ALBERT GOODWIN: The French Revolution TB/1064

CARLTON J. H. HAYES: A Generation of Materialism,
1871-1900.* *Illus.*   TB/3039

J. H. HEXTER: Reappraisals in History: *New Views on
History and Society in Early Modern Europe*
                                                     TB/1100

A. R. HUMPHREYS: The Augustan World: *Society,
Thought, and Letters in Eighteenth Century England*
                                                     TB/1105

HANS KOHN, Ed.: The Mind of Modern Russia: *Historical and Political Thought of Russia's Great Age*
                                                     TB/1065

SIR LEWIS NAMIER: Vanished Supremacies: *Essays on
European History, 1812-1918*°   TB/1088

JOHN U. NEF: Western Civilization Since the Renaissance: *Peace, War, Industry, and the Arts* TB/1113

FREDERICK L. NUSSBAUM: The Triumph of Science
and Reason, 1660-1685.* *Illus.*   TB/3009

RAYMOND W. POSTGATE, Ed.: Revolution from
1789 to 1906: *Selected Documents*   TB/1063

PENFIELD ROBERTS: The Quest for Security, 1715-
1740.* *Illus.*   TB/3016

PRISCILLA ROBERTSON: Revolutions of 1848: *A Social History*   TB/1025

ALBERT SOREL: Europe Under the Old Regime. *Translated by Francis H. Herrick*   TB/1121

N. N. SUKHANOV: The Russian Revolution, 1917:
Eyewitness Account. Edited by Joel Carmichael
Vol. I TB/1066; Vol. II TB/1067

JOHN B. WOLF: The Emergence of the Great Powers,
1685-1715.* *Illus.* TB/3010

JOHN B. WOLF: France: 1814-1919: *The Rise of a
Liberal-Democratic Society* TB/3019

Intellectual History

HERSCHEL BAKER: The Image of Man: *A Study of
the Idea of Human Dignity in Classical Antiquity, the
Middle Ages, and the Renaissance* TB/1047

J. BRONOWSKI & BRUCE MAZLISH: The Western
Intellectual Tradition: *From Leonardo to Hegel*
TB/3001

ERNST CASSIRER: The Individual and the Cosmos in
Renaissance Philosophy. *Translated with an Introduction by Mario Domandi* TB/1097

NORMAN COHN: The Pursuit of the Millennium:
*Revolutionary Messianism in medieval and Reforma-
tion Europe and its bearing on modern Leftist and
Rightist totalitarian movements* TB/1037

ARTHUR O. LOVEJOY: The Great Chain of Being: *A
Study of the History of an Idea* TB/1009

ROBERT PAYNE: Hubris: *A Study of Pride. Foreword
by Sir Herbert Read* TB/1031

BRUNO SNELL: The Discovery of the Mind: *The Greek
Origins of European Thought* TB/1018

ERNEST LEE TUVESON. Millennium and Utopia. *A
Study in the Background of the Idea of Progress.‖
New Preface by the Author* ● TB/1134

Literature, Poetry, The Novel & Criticism

JAMES BAIRD: Ishmael: *The Art of Melville in the
Contexts of International Primitivism* TB/1023

JACQUES BARZUN: The House of Intellect TB/1051

W. J. BATE: From Classic to Romantic: *Premises of
Taste in Eighteenth Century England* TB/1036

RACHEL BESPALOFF: On the Iliad TB/2006

R. P. BLACKMUR et al.: Lectures in Criticism. *Introduction by Huntington Cairns* TB/2003

ABRAHAM CAHAN: The Rise of David Levinsky: *a
novel. Introduction by John Higham* TB/1028

ERNST R. CURTIUS: European Literature and the Latin
Middle Ages TB/2015

GEORGE ELIOT: Daniel Deronda: *a novel. Introduction
by F. R. Leavis* TB/1039

ETIENNE GILSON: Dante and Philosophy TB/1089

ALFRED HARBAGE: As They Liked It: *A Study of
Shakespeare's Moral Artistry* TB/1035

STANLEY R. HOPPER, Ed.: Spiritual Problems in Contemporary Literature§ TB/21

A. R. HUMPHREYS: The Augustan World: *Society,
Thought, and Letters in Eighteenth Century England*°
TB/1105

ALDOUS HUXLEY: Antic Hay & The Gioconda Smile.°
Introduction by Martin Green TB/3503

HENRY JAMES: Roderick Hudson: *a novel. Introduction by Leon Edel* TB/1016

HENRY JAMES: The Tragic Muse: *a novel. Introduction by Leon Edel* TB/1017

ARNOLD KETTLE: An Introduction to the English
Novel. Volume I: *Defoe to George Eliot* TB/1011
Volume II: *Henry James to the Present* TB/1012

ROGER SHERMAN LOOMIS: The Development of
Arthurian Romance TB/1167

JOHN STUART MILL: On Bentham and Coleridge.
Introduction by F. R. Leavis TB/1070

PERRY MILLER & T. H. JOHNSON, Editors: The Puri-
tans: *A Sourcebook of Their Writings* Vol. I TB/1093
Vol. II TB/1094

KENNETH B. MURDOCK: Literature and Theology in
Colonial New England TB/99

SAMUEL PEPYS: The Diary of Samuel Pepys.° *Edited
by O. F. Morshead. Illus. by Ernest Shepard* TB/1007

ST.-JOHN PERSE: Seamarks TB/2002

O. E. RÖLVAAG: Giants in the Earth TB/3504

GEORGE SANTAYANA: Interpretations of Poetry and
Religion§ TB/9

C. P. SNOW: Time of Hope: *a novel* TB/1040

HEINRICH STRAUMANN: American Literature in the
Twentieth Century. *Revised Edition* TB/1168

DOROTHY VAN GHENT: The English Novel: *Form
and Function* TB/1050

E. B. WHITE: One Man's Meat. *Introduction by Walter
Blair* TB/3505

MORTON DAUWEN ZABEL, Editor: Literary Opinion
in America. Vol. I TB/3013; Vol. II TB/3014

Myth, Symbol & Folklore

JOSEPH CAMPBELL, Editor: Pagan and Christian Mysteries. *Illus.* TB/2013

MIRCEA ELIADE: Cosmos and History: *The Myth of
the Eternal Return*§ TB/2050

C. G. JUNG & C. KERÉNYI: Essays on a Science of
Mythology: *The Myths of the Divine Child and the
Divine Maiden* TB/2014

ERWIN PANOFSKY: Studies in Iconology: *Humanistic
Themes in the Art of the Renaissance. 180 illustrations* TB/1077

JEAN SEZNEC: The Survival of the Pagan Gods: *The
Mythological Tradition and its Place in Renaissance
Humanism and Art. 108 illustrations* TB/2004

HELLMUT WILHELM: Change: *Eight Lectures on the
I Ching* TB/2019

HEINRICH ZIMMER: Myths and Symbols in Indian
Art and Civilization. *70 illustrations* TB/2005

Philosophy

HENRI BERGSON: Time and Free Will: *An Essay on
the Immediate Data of Consciousness*° TB/1021

H. J. BLACKHAM: Six Existentialist Thinkers: *Kierke-
gaard, Nietzsche, Jaspers, Marcel, Heidegger, Sartre*°
TB/1002

ERNST CASSIRER: The Individual and the Cosmos in
Renaissance Philosophy. *Translated with an Introduction by Mario Domandi* TB/1097

ERNST CASSIRER: Rousseau, Kant and Goethe. *Introduction by Peter Gay* TB/1092

FREDERICK COPLESTON: Medieval Philosophy°
TB/376

A LETTER TO THE READER

Overseas, there is considerable belief
that we are a country of extreme conservatism and
that we cannot accommodate to social change.

Books about America in the hands of
readers abroad can help change those ideas.

The U. S. Information Agency cannot,
by itself, meet the vast need for books about
the United States.

You can help.

Harper Torchbooks provides three packets
of books on American history, economics,
sociology, literature and politics to
help meet the need.

To send a packet of Torchbooks [*] overseas,
all you need do is send your check for $7 (which
includes cost of shipping) to Harper & Row.
The U. S. Information Agency will distrib-
ute the books to libraries, schools, and other
centers all over the world.

I ask every American to support this
program, part of a worldwide BOOKS USA campaign.

I ask you to share in the opportunity to
help tell others about America.

EDWARD R. MURROW
Director,
U. S. Information Agency

[*retailing at $10.85 to $12.00]

PACKET I: *Twentieth Century America*

Dulles/America's Rise to World Power, 1898-1954
Cochran/The American Business System, 1900-1955
Zabel, Editor/Literary Opinion in America (two volumes)
Drucker/The New Society: *The Anatomy of Industrial Order*
Fortune Editors/America in the Sixties: *The Economy and the Society*

PACKET II: *American History*

Billington/The Far Western Frontier, 1830-1860
Mowry/The Era of Theodore Roosevelt and the
    Birth of Modern America, 1900-1912
Faulkner/Politics, Reform, and Expansion, 1890-1900
Cochran & Miller/The Age of Enterprise: *A Social History of
    Industrial America*
Tyler/Freedom's Ferment: *American Social History from the
    Revolution to the Civil War*

PACKET III: *American History*

Hansen/The Atlantic Migration, 1607-1860
Degler/Out of Our Past: *The Forces that Shaped Modern America*
Probst, Editor/The Happy Republic: *A Reader in Tocqueville's America*
Alden/The American Revolution, 1775-1783
Wright/The Cultural Life of the American Colonies, 1607-1763

*Your gift will be acknowledged directly to you by the overseas recipient.
Simply fill out the coupon, detach and mail with your check or money order.*

HARPER & ROW, PUBLISHERS · BOOKS USA DEPT.
49 East 33rd Street, New York 16, N. Y.

Packet I ☐   Packet II ☐   Packet III ☐

Please send the BOOKS USA library packet(s) indicated above, in my
name, to the area checked below. Enclosed is my remittance in the
amount of _____ for _____ packet(s) at $7.00 each.

_____ Africa   _____ Latin America

_____ Far East   _____ Near East

Name_____

Address_____

_____

NOTE: *This offer expires December 31, 1966.*